HIGH
MOUNTAIN
CHALLENGE

Seashells in My Pocket:
A Child's Guide to Exploring the Atlantic Coast from Maine to
North Carolina
Judith Hansen

At Timberline:
A Nature Guide to the Mountains of the Northeast
Frederic L. Steele

Forest and Crag:
A History of Hiking, Trail Blazing, and Adventure in the
Northeast Mountains
Laura and Guy Waterman

Lucy Crawford's History of the White Mountains
edited by Stearns Morse

Moving Mountains:
Coping with Change in Mountain Communities
Sara Neustadtl

AMC Maine Mountain Guide
6th Edition

AMC Massachusetts and Rhode Island Trail Guide
6th Edition

AMC White Mountain Guide
24th Edition

Hiking the Mountain State:
The Trails of West Virginia
Allen de Hart

North Carolina Hiking Trails
2nd Edition
Allen de Hart

HIGH MOUNTAIN CHALLENGE

A Guide for Young Mountaineers

LINDA BUCHANAN ALLEN

Appalachian Mountain Club Books
Boston

Cover illustration, text illustrations, and maps by Mary Trafton

Photographs by Linda Buchanan Allen (25, 109, 115, 126), Boyd Allen, III (14, 27, 39, 79, 88, 135, 160, back cover) and Jim Traverso (136)

Acknowledgments:
Special thanks to Jeff and Lois Hancock, Donald and Minnie Mae Murray, and Beth Frankel, for reading the manuscript; to Susan Cummings, Publisher, George Kane, Editor and Marketing Manager, and Gail Simon, Production Manager, at AMC Books; and to Jim Traverso, Ngorup Yondon Sherpa, Anu Sherpa, the staff at Overseas Adventure Travel, and the members of our climbing team, for a great adventure.

FIRST EDITION

HIGH MOUNTAIN CHALLENGE
A Guide for Young Mountaineers

©1989 by Linda Buchanan Allen

Published by Appalachian Mountain Club Books, 5 Joy St., Boston, MA 02108.
Distributed by The Talman Company, 150 Fifth Ave., New York, NY 10011.

Library of Congress Cataloging-in-Publication Data
Allen, Linda Buchanan, 1955–
    High mountain challenge: a guide for young mountaineers / Linda Buchanan
Allen.—1st ed.
        p.   cm.
    Bibliography: p.
    Summary: Chronicles an expedition the author made to Island Peak in Nepal and outlines the skills, equipment, and techniques used in mountain climbing.
        ISBN 0-910146-98-5 (alk. paper): $9.95
    1. Mountaineering—Juvenile literature. 2. Mountaineering—Nepal—Juvenile literature. 3. Nepal—Description and travel—Juvenile literature. [1. Mountaineering. 2. Nepal.] I. Title.
GV200.A44   1989
796.5′22′095496—dc19   89–16
                                                                          AC

The paper used in this publication meets the minimum requirements of the American National Standard for Information Sciences—Permanence of Paper for Printed Library Materials, ANSI Z39.48–1984.∞

Printed in the United States of America

10 9 8 7 6 5 4 3 2   90 91 92 93

FOR BOYD
Who followed his boyhood dream

Contents

    MOUNTAIN METHODS: When You Travel Far   189
        from Home

    Glossary: Tools, Techniques, Troubles, and   191
        Terrain
    Getting Started   195
    Just in Case (Your First-Aid Kit)   197
    For Further Reading   198
    About the Author   201
    About the AMC   203

Introduction:
A Trip with Tips

*H*igh *Mountain Challenge* is an adventure story, but it is also designed to help you get started in mountaineering. Many young people are learning to climb mountains. You can, too.

Each chapter of *High Mountain Challenge* provides you with information about mountaineering as part of the story. At the end of each chapter, a section called "Mountain Methods" gives you tips on a single aspect of mountain climbing that relates to the chapter. For example, the "Mountain Methods" section following chapter 1 tells you how to get in shape for mountaineering. That way, when you have finished reading the story, you can easily refer to the "Mountain Methods" later on for information about climbing.

At the end of the book, a glossary called "Tools, Techniques, Troubles, and Terrain" defines and describes special equipment and skills involved in mountaineering, as well as troubles such as avalanches and natural formations such as glaciers. "Getting Started" gives you the names and addresses of outdoor organizations that include young people in their membership, as well as outdoor-equipment stores with mail-order catalogs. It also tells you where to write for maps. The section called "Just in Case" tells you what to put in your first-aid kit. "For Further Reading" lists others books and magazines on mountain climbing.

Mountaineering has a special thrill and challenge requiring knowledge and practice along with the ability to deal safely with problems in the outdoors. Whether you plan only to climb a small mountain near your home or dream of becoming a world-class mountaineer, you can do it once you learn how. Turn the page and take your first steps.

1
Shakedown on
Mt. Washington

WIND POURED DOWN from the summit and slammed me
head on. I spun away from it, pulling my goggles down over my
face. Cyclones of snow whirled across the frozen alpine meadow;
particles of ice stung my mouth and cheeks. This was a perfect day
for climbing. My husband Boyd and I were lucky. Winds from the
top of Mt. Washington, in northern New Hampshire, were blowing at only about fifty miles per hour, and the sky was clear.

Winter climbing on Mt. Washington can be a nightmare. At
6,288 feet above sea level, Mt. Washington often has bad weather
and dangerous climbing conditions. Avalanches tumble down the
ravines, and winds have been recorded blasting over the summit at
two hundred miles per hour. Weather on Mt. Washington changes
very quickly. In just an hour or two, a beautiful sunny day can turn
into the kind of blinding storm a climber might easily get lost in.
The important thing to remember about climbing on Mt. Washington is to be prepared for anything.

We were on Mt. Washington for a special reason. Boyd and I
had each been backpacking and mountain climbing around the
United States for many years. Boyd started camping in the Boy
Scouts, and I started hiking during high school. Boyd had carried a
dream with him since his scouting days. "I want to see Mt. Everest," he told me, "and I want to climb a twenty-thousand-foot-
high mountain." I was game for the challenge.

On a map we found Nepal, the country where Mt. Everest lies.
Near Mt. Everest we located a 20,285-foot-high mountain called
Island Peak, which we thought we could climb.

Nepal is a small country halfway around the world from the
United States. It is five hundred miles long and 150 miles wide,
about the size and shape of California. India borders Nepal on its
southern side; Tibet (which is ruled by China) borders Nepal on its
northern side. Nepal is best known as the home of the Himalaya,
the highest mountains in the world. The entire Himalayan Range

1

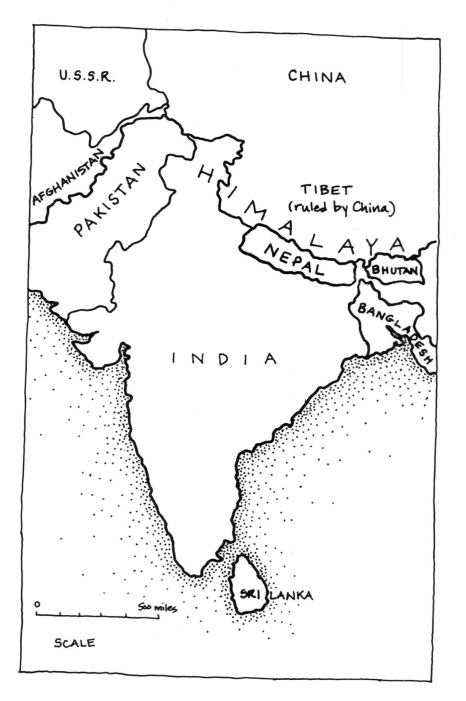

Nepal is bordered by India on its southern side and Tibet on its northern side.

stretches through Tibet, Nepal, India, and Pakistan. But the most famous single Himalayan mountain is in Nepal: Mt. Everest. At 29,028 feet above sea level, it is the tallest mountain on earth.

Mountaineers from many parts of the world go to Nepal to climb the Himalayan peaks. People also travel to Nepal to trek (or hike) along the mountain paths and to meet the people who live among the mountains. On our expedition, we would do both. Boyd and I signed up with an agency that made all the travel arrangements and provided a guide to lead us, along with several other people, on our expedition.

Long before we reached Nepal we started getting in shape, and an important part of training was climbing Mt. Washington.

We arrived at the base of Mt. Washington early on that bright winter day in February, nine months before our scheduled trip to Island Peak. We dropped our packs in the snow and checked inside them to make certain we had everything we needed. First, plenty of water. It was important to carry at least two quarts of water each and to remember to drink it often along the trail. (We didn't want to eat snow because it could lower our body temperatures, making us cold.) The body loses its water supply very quickly in the winter, through hard breathing in the cold air and through sweat. We slid an extra sock over each water bottle and buried them part way into the pack to keep the water from freezing. Then we checked our extra clothing and food. I pulled a small nylon stuff-sack out of my pack, filled with cheese, pepperoni wrapped in plastic, flat pita bread, two oranges, several granola bars, and a couple of chocolate bars. I slipped a chocolate bar and a granola bar into the front pouch of my anorak (a pullover windbreaker with a hood). I nibbled at these from time to time as I walked along the trail so as not to run out of energy.

In the bottom of my backpack I stored a winter parka, extra mittens, extra socks, an extra sweater, a headlamp, toilet paper, butane lighter, candles, and some first-aid items. I placed the food near the top of the pack, within easy reach. In his pack, Boyd carried more emergency gear: a climbing rope, a small camp stove, a sleeping bag, more first-aid items, a map, and extra clothing. All of these things made our backpacks heavy, but if we were caught in a storm we would be glad we had them! We each also had a compass and a Swiss Army knife. To the outside of our packs we had strapped crampons (metal spikes that attach to climbing boots to help grip the snow and ice) and ice axes, both of which would help anchor us to the steep slopes higher up the mountain.

We zipped up our packs, hoisted them onto our shoulders, and started up the snowy trail. Boyd strode ahead of me, his long legs churning through the deep white powder. Along the sides of the trail, snow slid from pine boughs with a sigh. Up ahead rose our destination: the bright white summit shouldering a dark blue sky. Veins of dark rock stood out on the summit cone; plumes of snow floated off the summit.

Mt. Washington is only one-third the height of Island Peak, I thought, *and still it looks like a tough climb.*

New snow clung to my heavy mountaineering boots as I shuffled along, adjusting the pack on my shoulders. I rested my hands on my waist so that my lungs had more room to breathe. We stopped often to drink water and eat snacks. Once in a while we took out the trail map to see where we were and how far we had to go. It was a magnificent day, and we were moving along at a strong pace. I had no doubts that we would reach the summit.

Suddenly the trail seemed to climb straight to the sky. We were at the base of the steep incline that leads up to Lion's Head, the huge bulge of rock over which we'd have to climb to reach the alpine meadow and then the summit cone (the cone-shaped slope leading to the summit). We dropped our packs in the snow and unstrapped our crampons from the sides. The trail was so steep and slippery I did not know how I could bend over and balance on one foot to get my crampons strapped on. I struggled with them a while, leaning against a rock with one hand and lifting my downhill foot for a second at a time until I got my boot fitted into the crampon and the straps pulled tight over the toe of the boot and around my ankles. I made sure that the straps were secure, for we would be walking in deep snow and over rock for several hours, and the crampons would take a beating.

Next came the ice ax. I would always hold the ax in my uphill hand, changing hands if I changed direction. This would help me keep my balance. So I slipped my uphill mitten through the ax strap and twirled it around to keep the strap from sliding off my hand.

An ice ax is one of the most important tools that a mountaineer carries. It's about two feet long, with a point at the bottom and a flat head on top. The mountaineer can use it like a short cane,

Winter climbing requires special clothing and gear to fight the wind and cold. Crampons and an ice ax help the climber grip the steep slope of snow.

balancing against it while walking up a steep slope. Or it can be used like a hammer to hack into the ice and provide handholds. And, when used the right way in a fall, it can save a mountaineer's life. Proper use of an ice ax is not a guarantee of safety, but it can improve the odds of surviving a fall the way a seatbelt can improve the odds for someone in a car accident.

Boyd changed from his regular glasses to his sunglasses. I swung my pack onto my shoulders and started slowly up the steep trail. I looked upward: all I could see was a steep, narrow, snowy trail. Sometimes the trail was a wall of snow, and I chopped at it with my ice ax, kicking the front of my cramponed boot into the wall and hauling myself up. Sometimes I clambered over huge tree roots and rocks covered with thin ice. I was concentrating so hard on making each step that I did not know how fast we were going or how far we were from the top.

I turned a corner on the trail and a slash of blue sky appeared above me. We were coming out of the woods, up over the top of Lion's Head. Voices drifted down from the distance above; there was a group ahead of us.

Plant the ax, step, step; plant the ax, step, step. Slowly, I trudged up toward the clearing, across bare rock, then onto wind-blown, crusty snow. Breathing hard, leaning on my ax, I turned around to watch Boyd, who was following. Steadily, the red shirt came toward me.

Beyond us, the White Mountains stretched into the distance, hushed and serene. Tiny skiers trickled down the slopes of Wildcat Mountain, straight across from Mt. Washington. As Boyd came up over the bulge of Lion's Head, I greeted him and then turned to look across the frozen alpine meadow to the summit cone. The group ahead of us, spread out across the meadow, moved one by one onto the cone. For the first time, I looked at my watch. We had been on the mountain for five hours.

"Let's stop for a snack," I suggested. Boyd nodded, and we moved over to some rocks warmed by the sun. Slowly, I lowered myself to sit. My legs were beginning to tire. I sat cross-legged on the rock and sliced cheese and pepperoni, stuffed both into cold swatches of pita bread, and handed a sandwich to Boyd. Wind billowed up from below. Off the cliff, a hawk floated over Tuckerman Ravine.

Boyd looked across the alpine meadow and said thoughtfully, "You know, we may not make it today."

Startled, I asked, "What do you mean? All we have to do is cross the alpine meadow and then we're on the summit cone. From there it's not far to the top."

He swallowed the last of his sandwich and took a sip from the water bottle. Snow crystals formed on his red mustache. "It's taken us five hours to get this far. The alpine meadow is wider than it looks and the summit cone is pretty steep. It could take us another three hours to reach the top. And remember, we still have to get down."

I stood up, shoved the stuff-sack with remaining food into my pack, and tried to tease him out of his doubts.

"Don't be silly," I said lightly. "We'll make it. You'll see." Feeling stronger with the food in me, I stood up and headed off over the rocky surface of Lion's Head, toward the frozen meadow.

As I walked along the rocks, my crampons skidded, scraping the surface like chalk down a blackboard. Then I stepped into the meadow. Wind hissed across the hard snow. I walked two steps on the crust, then one foot shot down below the surface, knee deep. Two steps, break through. Three steps, break through. This was going to be tedious walking. I looked around at the meadow and the base of the summit cone. We had hiked Mt. Washington during the summer, so I knew the landmarks. Yet they were strange when covered with snow and ice. It was as if I were climbing a mountain that I had dreamed of sometime long ago—a mountain strange, yet somehow familiar.

As we approached the base of the summit cone, the wind blew stronger. Cold swirled around us in little cyclones. I thought of climbers who had been blown right off the mountain in winter.

I leaned against a rock for a short rest and took two bites of a granola bar from the pouch of my anorak. Boyd moved on ahead of me. We started the climb upward onto the cone, making zig-zags across its face. The wind now hammered so hard we had to shout to each other to speed up or slow down. I leaned into the mountain, planting my ice ax as deeply as I could in the crusty snow, afraid I would be torn off by the wind and go tumbling back down toward the meadow. I came to the base of a steep, smooth boulder. Scrub pine and light snow surrounded it. I knew that if I stepped into that snow near the scrub, I'd sink into a "spruce hole"—a natural trap of snow and air that lies near a bush or tree. I tried to reach the top of the rock with my hands and pull myself up. I slipped off. I tried my crampons on the rock. They slid off too. I was stuck. Boyd was already ahead of me, out of sight. I shouted to him. Wind slammed the shout back into my face. I leaned against the rock in frustration. Then I found the spot where the snow joined the rock and dug in my ice ax above my head. I kicked my left crampon through the crust and pulled myself up along the rock. I rested my right crampon against the boulder and boosted myself further. Soon I scrambled up over the top.

Nearly two-thirds of the way up the summit cone, we took our last break. Boyd looked at his watch again and shook his head. "We've been on the mountain over six hours. It is three o'clock now, and it will take us at least three hours to get back down off the mountain. I think we should turn around."

I looked up toward the summit. The group ahead of us was going to reach it. This was a magnificent day: brilliant sky, good climbing conditions. I wanted so badly to stand on the summit in winter. But I knew Mt. Washington. If we tried for the top this late in the day, we would have to cross the alpine meadow in twilight and climb down much of Lion's Head in darkness. Climbing down is no easier than climbing up; it requires concentration and good leg strength. Late in the day, both of these can be in short supply. A mistake could end in an accident.

"OK," I grumbled. My disappointment showed, but I knew that safe climbing involved making decisions such as this.

We turned around and hiked back down the summit cone, across the alpine meadow, and to the edge of Lion's Head. After a quick sip of water and a bite of chocolate, we began our descent of the steep trail. Going down, I leaned way over to drive my ice ax deep into the snow as an anchor. It slipped way in, almost to the head of the ax. Then I took two steps, wriggled the ax out of the snow, and planted it again. Soon my back began to ache from leaning over with the weight of the pack sliding up toward my neck. The snow was deep and slippery. Clumps balled up among the claws of my crampons and I stopped periodically to kick the icy snow loose. The trail was so steep that my knees felt like taffy being pulled apart with each step I took. After two hours, they began to wobble.

Mountaineering is nothing but hard work, I thought to myself.

Suddenly I heard a *whoosh*—and another climber came sailing down the trail on his behind! Carrying his ice ax across his chest and whistling happily, he slid past me and on down the trail, in a technique called the glissade.

Gradually, daylight drained from the sky and the woods. The chill of dusk drifted into my muscles and bones. I was tired. Finally, the trail began to level out. We reached the bottom of Lion's Head and arrived at the base of Mt. Washington as the last light left the sky. Behind us, the summit stood ghostly and quiet.

As I walked the last part of the trail, I thought of some of the great mountaineers who had tried to climb Mt. Everest and other mountains in the Himalaya. In 1953, two members of a British expedition—a New Zealand climber named Edmund Hillary and his partner from Nepal, Tenzing Norgay—became the first people to stand on the summit of Mt. Everest. Since then, many other men and women have climbed Mt. Everest. The first American expedition claimed the summit in 1963. Junko Tabei, a member of the Japanese women's expedition in 1975, was the first woman to climb Mt. Everest. And in 1988, Stacy Marie Allison became the first American woman to reach the top. But many years before these expeditions, another mountaineer, George Leigh Mallory, tried to climb Mt. Everest. In 1924, Mallory and his partner were last seen by other expedition members far in the distance, making their way slowly along a high ridge. Then clouds drifted over them. When the clouds cleared, Mallory and his partner were gone. No one knows whether they died on their way up to the summit or on their way down; no one knows whether they made it to the top. Mallory was once asked why he wanted to climb Mt. Everest and he answered, "because it is there." But when he said this, he did not mean that Mt. Everest existed and therefore he must climb it. He meant that Everest was "there," just beyond his reach.

We needed these months, far ahead of our own expedition, to practice winter climbing so that Island Peak would be within our grasp. Later in the winter, we practiced technical ice climbing (climbing with ropes) and camping in snow. When warm weather arrived, we hiked and backpacked. Hiking long distances up and downhill at high altitudes would be hard on our hearts and lungs. To strengthen them, we took aerobic fitness classes at the local YMCA several times a week. There, we ran in place, while doing exercises with our arms and legs. On days when we did not have classes, we went running through the outskirts of our town. We rode our bikes long distances, to work our leg muscles as well as our hearts and lungs. We ran up and down the bleachers at the high school football field. In addition, we did pushups, situps, and leg lifts. Every muscle needed to be strong, for we would depend on those muscles while climbing in the Himalaya. Preparations took months. But by November, we were ready—and determined—to climb among the highest mountains in the world.

MOUNTAIN METHODS
Getting in Shape for Mountaineering

One of the most important parts of mountaineering is what you do *before* you get to the mountain. Good fitness prepares you for long walks, difficult weather, and carrying gear. Start getting in shape as far in advance as you can. Begin slowly with a few exercises and short distances; then build up. You can do most of your getting in shape right at home.

Walking

Remember that most of mountaineering is walking. Walk as much as you can. If you have a small backpack, fill it with books and carry it while you are taking a long walk (at least an hour).

Aerobic Exercises

Aerobic exercises strengthen your heart and lungs. To benefit from aerobic exercise, you need to increase your heart rate (how fast your heart beats) for twenty minutes at least three times a week. Ask your gym teacher or doctor how fast your heart should beat when you are exercising.

Some of the best aerobic exercises are running, swimming, bicycling, and cross-country skiing. You can even run up and down a flight of stairs or the bleachers at your local football field. You can get aerobic exercise by taking fitness classes as well. If your school doesn't have aerobic fitness classes, ask your gym teacher where you might take them, or call a local YMCA or YWCA. If you can ride your bike to school or to fitness class, you'll get even more exercise.

Muscle-strengthening Exercises

To strengthen your muscles, do exercises such as situps, pushups, and leg lifts. Start with a few (for example, twenty situps, five pushups, and five leg lifts); then build up to more. Do these at least three times a week. Strong muscles will help you carry a backpack, walk long distances, and use any tools you may need while climbing.

2
Festival of Light

THE SMALL PLANE DIPPED slightly to the left, and the great mountains came into view: Dhaulagiri, Annapurna, Manaslu. They shimmered in the distance, through the haze. We had traveled for two days without stopping. Now we were eleven thousand miles from home.

The Nepalese stewardess ducked into the passenger cabin and announced that we were approaching the international airport at Kathmandu (Kat-mahn-doo), the capital of Nepal. The plane positioned itself far above the airstrip and then nosed down onto the black runway, bouncing to a stop in the bright sun. Outside the terminal, people waited to greet passengers. I unfolded myself from my seat and slipped out into the sunlight. My legs were wobbly; I was tired, but excited. I pushed my backpack along the worn counter at customs. "Mountain climbing," I said, when the customs officer asked why I was visiting Nepal.

Jim, our American guide, emerged from the crowd. "Welcome!" he called and reached out his hand to shake ours. He was thin and wiry with dark, curly hair. He herded us out into the parking lot, where our duffels were already stacked in the dirt. He packed us into a tiny, ancient cab, stuffed the duffels in the trunk, and gave the driver directions to our hotel. The driver sped off. Reeling around people, other cars, and animals, the cab tore through dirt streets, with the open trunk lid waving and slapping the bags at each bump we bounced over. We passed an old woman dressed in brown rags, shuffling along alone; a man riding a bicycle across a dry field, a banner of dust rising from the back wheel of the bike; loose cows wandering everywhere; people on rooftops; and one young Nepalese soldier leaning out of his barracks window. We had arrived.

We checked into the Yak & Yeti Hotel and then gathered in the lobby for our first meeting. The climbing team had arrived on different flights, from different parts of the United States. We settled into large, comfortable leather chairs and eyed each other as Jim introduced us. We shook hands, wanting to like each other right away. The group included George, who worked in Yellowstone Park in Wyoming; Allen, from Seattle; Linda and Jerry, postal workers from Ohio; Jimmy, who lived near our own town in Massachusetts; and Boyd and me. This was the team. We would be together for the next five weeks. We had to get along.

"First, I'll give you some information about Kathmandu—where to shop, where to eat, and what to see—since we'll be here for a couple of days before leaving for the mountains," said Jim. "Tonight, we'll eat dinner together here at the hotel, and we'll have our first briefing about the climb." After handing us sheets of paper with facts about Kathmandu, he answered questions about Nepalese money, shops, and customs that we should try to follow. Then, in late afternoon, we set off to see the city's sights.

We had arrived during the celebration of Diwali (Dih-wahl-ee), the Festival of Light. During this five-day festival, people place candles in the doorways of their homes and shops, honor dogs and cows (which have special meaning in Nepalese culture), and worship the goddess Lakshmi (Lahk-shmee), who is the Hindu goddess of wealth. On the last day of Diwali, sisters honor their brothers by doing special favors for them and paying special attention to them.

Exploring the streets of the Thamel (Tah-mel) district, we saw richly colored rugs, jewelry, and sweaters hanging outside the shops. A beautiful sweater attracted my attention. I took it into the shop to bargain for it with the shopkeeper.

"Kattiko parchha?" I asked.

"Two hundred rupees," he answered. I thought quickly. In Nepalese currency, twenty rupees is about equal to one dollar. Ten dollars for that sweater was a low price by American standards, but in Nepal, you bargain for everything.

"One hundred fifty," I countered.

"One hundred seventy-five," he said. I bought the sweater.

We wandered through the maze of streets as evening drew into the city. Colorful flags and banners were strung from house to house, children tossed firecrackers and sparklers into the dirt streets, people chanted and sang. Dark, lean faces peered out from doorways and windows; a boy pounded a wet pair of jeans in the water at the side of the road in an effort to get them clean. Children marched

Thamel district, Kathmandu. Trekkers and townspeople watch as a group of boys celebrate the final day of Diwali by riding on top of a bus.

through the streets thumping hollow drums that we could hear blocks away. Cows (which are sacred to the people who follow the Hindu religion and are allowed to roam loose) ambled along, nosing trash for morsels of food. A young shopkeeper lit a row of candles outside his jewelry store, ready for evening business. A little girl with wild, dark hair gripped the hand of her younger sister. Four boys crowded into the doorway of a shop to sing for money; the shopkeeper shooed them away. A gong sounded. A firecracker exploded nearby. Mountaineering, I was beginning to realize, can be much more than just climbing a mountain. It can mean traveling far from home, meeting people who live differently, learning new customs, and eating new food.

Later, in the hotel restaurant, a waiter asked, "What will you have, *memsahib?*" (mem-sahb) He stood at the end of the table, waiting for me to answer. "*Thali* (thahl-ee), please," I said. He nodded. Twenty minutes later I received a large tin platter filled with rice, curry, spinach, cheese, and *chappattis* (chah-pah-teez), thin cakes like tortillas or pita bread. This was my first meal in

Nepal. Jim showed me how to eat *thali:* I ripped a piece of a *chappatti,* cupped it in my fingers, and scooped up the spice or sauce I wanted. It was delicious.

At dinner, Jim talked about the trek to Island Peak. We would fly from Kathmandu to a small village called Lukla (Look-la), at 9,200 feet above sea level; then we would begin a two-week walk to Island Peak, with a few days of rest along the way so that we could get used to the high altitude. He explained that the itinerary was planned carefully, with flexibility built in to allow for any delays or bad weather. He told us what kind of maps to buy so that we could trace a clear route along the trail to Island Peak. We discussed how far we would walk each day and what type of terrain we would cover. Jim explained that before we even checked out of the hotel, he would examine all our gear to make sure that we had everything we needed. We would not have much chance to replace anything once we left Kathmandu. We left dinner excited and anxious to get to the mountains, realizing that even though we had checked and double-checked our plans before leaving the United States, it was important to check them once again.

The following day we were free to sightsee around Kathmandu. Boyd and I hired a guide named Kiran to take us to some of the city's special places and explain them to us. Nepal is filled with people of many different backgrounds and customs, although most people in Nepal follow either the Hindu or Buddhist religion. Nepal is the only kingdom in the world where Hinduism is the official religion. Kiran, who was born a Hindu, would like to switch his religion to Buddhism. "But it is against the law," he said. (People who are born Hindus are not allowed to change their religion.)

People who practice Hinduism worship many different gods that all lead to one god, Brahma, the Supreme Being. Hindus must follow strict customs and rules of social class. People who practice Buddhism worship the god Buddha, who teaches kindness and tolerance of others. Buddhism is not quite as strict as Hinduism. Followers of both religions believe in reincarnation, which means that when a person dies, he or she is reborn as another person or even as an animal. That way, a person never really dies. About 90 percent of the Nepalese people are Hindu, while only about 10 percent are Buddhist. Hinduism and Buddhism often overlap and mix; many Buddhist temples also have monuments to Hindu gods, as we were about to see.

Kiran took us past the royal palace, where the king and queen of Nepal live, and outside the town, up a steep hill to a Buddhist temple called Swayambhunath (Swy-am-boo-nath), or the Temple of Monkeys. As we got out of the cab, monkeys swarmed around us, on the paths, in the trees, in and out of the buildings of the temple. Although Swayambhunath is mostly a Buddhist temple, monkeys are important symbols of worship in the Hindu religion. Swayambhunath, just like the two religions it represents, is very old: it became a religious site about 2,500 years ago.

"People live here," explained Kiran, pointing to the run-down buildings that surrounded the temple. The windows had no glass, there was no electricity, and the people did not have running water or heat. (Most houses in Nepal lack these things.) "A whole family may live in two rooms. Since people are not allowed to buy property in a temple, families pass their apartments from generation to generation as gifts."

We left Swayambhunath and drove to the other side of Kathmandu to see Bodhnath (Bahd-nath), the largest Buddhist temple in Nepal. We climbed the steps to its enormous white dome late in the afternoon. Kiran pointed past one of the statues outside the temple to a giant mountain shimmering in the distance. "Ganesh Himal," he said; it was one of the great Himalayan peaks. We stepped inside the temple, where a huge gold statue of Buddha, studded with precious stones, filled the room. Candles made of butter flickered in the low light. Bright red and gold tapestries lined the ceiling. The Nepalese people, no matter how poor, would never steal the stones or jewels in this temple; it is open at all times.

The following morning we got up early, lugged our heavy duffels into the hotel lobby, packed them into cabs, and set off for the airport to fly to Lukla. As we hurtled through the early-morning mist, we passed a huge blue bus that had slid off the road and was now wedged into the bank beside the road. A cow lay next to it, twisted on its back, feet up, tongue hanging out. People milled around aimlessly; no one seemed to know what to do. But according to the Hindu religion, a terrible crime had been committed: a bus driver had struck and killed a sacred cow.

We arrived at the terminal, checked in, passed through security, and were told that our flight was canceled because of fog. Pilots who fly to the mountains fly only in good weather since they have no computers or other instruments to help them find their way. We turned around and headed back to the hotel to wait for a chance to fly the following day. We were disappointed, but we knew we could have fun exploring the city again that afternoon.

The next day we packed up and tried again. Once more, it was foggy. We sat and waited. Finally, there was some activity. George, whose duffel was the lightest, could have a spot on the first flight out. We sat around a small table on a balcony above the main room, where we could keep an eye on what was going on below. Jim bustled back and forth, gesturing, speaking in Nepali, trying to get us seats on a flight. A Nepalese woman made herself comfortable on my duffel, next to the luggage scale. Several Nepalese men, in uniform but with no apparent duties, crouched on their haunches on top of the security counter. About a hundred people crowded below—frustrated trekkers and climbers, mountain guides, and people waiting to go home to the mountains. In Nepal, no matter how carefully you plan, things change.

Finally, Jim cupped his hands to his mouth and shouted, "George! Get down here! You're leaving now!" George leapt from his seat, his glasses bouncing off the bridge of his nose. He straightened them and bounded downstairs. We were making progress. One of us was on the way.

Then all further fights were canceled for the day. Dejected, we collected our gear, trudged out to the parking lot, and once again climbed into a cab to head back to the city. No one spoke. The noise and crowds of the city were beginning to close in on us. We had seen the sights. And from the city, we could see the mountains; we just couldn't seem to get there.

That afternoon, we all decided to take a short hike outside the city to stretch our legs and see some of the countryside. If we couldn't get to the mountains, at least we could get to the hills. We set off on a narrow path surrounded by rice paddies and fields of gain. Children, suddenly aware of us, scampered up from the fields, shouting "Hello! Bye-bye!"

We waved and answered, "Hello! Bye-bye!"

We passed several families working together in one field, with scythes and an ancient threshing machine operated by foot pedals, like a bicycle. Most people in Nepal are farmers, and most farming is done by hand or with the help of animals; there are no huge tractors or other modern farm machines.

We spent another night in Kathmandu, desperately hoping that the next day would be our lucky day. The following morning, we were met at the airport with the same scene as the days before: fog and a throng of frustrated travelers. We took our regular seats to watch and wait. Jim went to work on the authorities. The fog began to lift. Then, his call came: "Everyone! Get down here!" We scrambled downstairs, through security, and out onto the runway.

We were off to the mountains.

MOUNTAIN METHODS

Planning Your Mountaineering Trip

Planning a mountaineering trip includes choosing where you want to go and for how long; studying the trail map; considering how you will get to and from the mountain; and deciding what to take. Planning also includes thinking about the unexpected.

1. When you decide where you want to go, you need to think about how much time you have to make your trip. Do you plan to climb the mountain in one day, or is this an overnight trip? How long will it take to get to the mountain? How many miles do you plan to hike?

2. Study a map or guidebook before you go, even if you have climbed this mountain before. What type of terrain will you be climbing? Is the trail steep and rocky or is it smooth and gradual? Consider an alternate route in case the trail you have chosen is impassable. (It might be flooded or no longer in use.)

3. Plan to make your trip with a partner. When you are on the trail, you may be far away from other people. If one person gets lost or hurt, the other can provide first aid or go for help. Discuss transportation to and from the mountain. And before you leave, let someone at home know where you are going and when you plan to be back.

4. If the mountain is far from where you live and you are uncertain about the weather on or near the mountain, call the park or forest service closest to it. Never *start* a mountaineering trip in bad weather.

5. Think about how you will deal with the unexpected— an injury, a sudden storm, or the climb simply taking

longer than you'd planned. Discuss these possibilities and some solutions with your climbing partner.

6. See the next three chapters' "Mountain Methods," "The Right Stuff: What to Take on Your Mountaineering Trip," "What to Eat on Your Mountaineering Trip," and "What to Wear on Your Mountaineering Trip."

3
"The Clouds Have Rocks in Them"

THE NEPALESE PILOTS SAY, "The clouds have rocks in them." As I stood on the runway waiting my turn to board the plane, I understood what they meant. Sun burned through the haze and the great white peaks shimmered in the distance. I rested on one foot, then on the other, impatiently. I couldn't bear anything to stop us now.

The ground crew lowered the staircase from the plane, and we climbed the rickety stairs, one by one. I squeezed into the tiny cabin, which held only ten passengers, and found a seat. I jammed my pack next to me. Boyd forced himself and his pack into the seat ahead of me, right behind the cockpit. I pressed my hand against the window, just above the wing of the plane. Jimmy, Allen, Jerry, and Linda settled themselves throughout the cabin of the plane; Jim sat across from me, in front.

The pilots revved the engine and the plane rocked back and forth with the force of the propellers. They put on their head-phones, flipped switches, and turned dials on the dashboard of the cockpit. Then the pilot pulled the throttle and the plane inched forward along the runway. The engine buzzed even louder and we began to roll, faster and faster, gaining speed, until the nose lifted and we were aloft, climbing steep into the sky. A sharp turn, and we were headed to the mountains.

I gripped my pack with excitement and looked down. Below, the tropical green of the valley gave way to pale green hills crisscrossed by trails. We hung suspended above Nepal, hovering like an insect. The plane chugged along. The pilot and copilot set their dials and took off their headphones. The pilot settled down to read the morning paper. Our stewardess, dressed in a long tunic, passed a tray of hard candies wrapped in cellophane. I unwrapped one and popped it in my mouth. The sticky sweetness spread through my mouth.

Then the plane dipped a little and the big mountains came into view, brilliant against the blue sky: Nuptse (Nuhp-tsee), 25,771 feet high; Lhotse (Low-tsee), 27,940 feet high; and Everest, 29,028 feet high. A chill rippled through me. Everest was there, pulling me toward it like a magnet. For the next two weeks, we would be walking toward it. After that, we would walk away from it. Everything we did would take place in relation to Everest. It would be a presence in our lives for nearly a month. Here, ahead of us, lay the first part of Boyd's dream: to see Mt. Everest. Excitedly, he leaned forward into the cockpit and snapped a picture of the mountain. Then the plane veered slightly and Everest was gone from sight, blocked by mountains that were smaller but closer. We would not see it again until the following day.

The pilot folded his newspaper and swung back to the dials on the dashboard. Both men put on their headphones. The plane jolted slightly to the right and I looked down. Far, far below lay a thin ribbon of dirt: the runway at Lukla. The pilot pointed the nose of the plane at the runway and dove.

I clutched my pack and the back of the seat in front of me, my heart drifting up into my throat. The plane clattered and shook. Then the nose came up suddenly and we touched down, bouncing up the runway to a stop.

The stewardess flipped open the hatch and scurried down the steps to the ground. Slowly, we each unfolded ourselves and pressed down the aisle with our packs held ahead of us, emerging into sunlight. Everything was chaos. Each day when the planes come, the people of Lukla clear the livestock and children off the runway and then stand around the hill above the airstrip, watching to see who comes and goes. There were waves and shouts in many languages. Someone tossed our duffels on the ground in the dust. Then the pilots collected their payload of passengers returning to Kathmandu, loaded up, spun the plane around, and headed back down the runway. In a cloud of dust, the plane lifted off the ground toward the sun, veered, and floated away.

We stood around, confused. We had come to the Khumbu (Koom-boo), the land of the Sherpa people, whose guests we would be for the next month, as we roamed among their villages and along their trails. Sherpas are refugees from Tibet, which borders Nepal to the northeast. (Sherpa means "person from the east.") When China invaded Tibet in 1950, many Sherpas fled across the border, over the mountains, and into Nepal. During the early 1900's, when British climbers went to Tibet to explore and begin attempts to climb Everest from the north, they enlisted Sherpas to help carry the loads. Since then, Sherpas have worked for and with many mountaineering expeditions. Some have become accomplished climbers. When Edmund Hillary reached the summit of Everest in 1953, his partner was a Sherpa named Tenzing Norgay. The Sherpas are devout Buddhists, and along the trail we would see the prayer flags and prayer wheels of Buddhism.

All around us, as we stood on the airstrip, we heard the traditional greeting, "Namaste!" (nah-mah-stay), which means "I salute the holiness in you." Nepalese people say this to mean "hello," "good-bye," and "how are you." Then we heard a familiar voice: George shouted and jogged down the hill to meet us.

Gradually, we sorted through the piles of stuff on the ground and dragged our duffels to the side of the airstrip. Jim counted heads, then duffels. A circle of Sherpas gathered. He spoke to them in Nepali, nodding his head and gesturing. Nepali was the language they shared. All Sherpas speak their native tribal language, but many also speak Nepali, the national language; some even speak a little English. We hauled the heavy gear into a heap and then walked down a small path to a low stone building I hadn't noticed before, right at the side of the airstrip. Gradually, cattle and people drifted back across the runway. Most of the cattle were yaks, the beasts of burden in eastern Nepal. Yaks look a bit like oxen, with long, thick, wiry fur and large horns. They carry loads along the trail, from village to village, for traders and mountaineers. Since there are no cars or roads in the Khumbu, people count on yaks to get their belongings from one place to another. The wheel has not yet come to Khumbu for two reasons: one, it would be nearly impossible to build a road through the Himalaya; two, the circle, or wheel, has special meaning to Buddhists and should not be used to roll along the ground.

"This is the hotel of a friend of mine," Jim said, gesturing to the building. "Let's have something to eat." We arranged ourselves around a wooden table set on the lawn, slipping on our glacier glasses (special sunglasses) to block the blazing sun.

Jim turned and pointed to the mountain behind us. "That's my ridge," he announced, barely concealing his pride. "My friends and I made a first ascent of it—we were the first to climb it." The cold, sharp ridge angled across the sky to the summit of Kwangde (Kwang-day), at 19,720 feet above sea level.

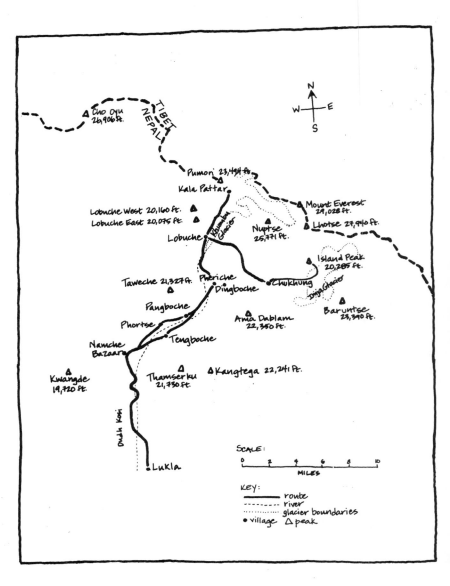

The Khumbu region of Nepal is the home of the Sherpas and Mt. Everest. Use this map as you follow the story.

A yak, loaded with trekking and climbing gear, plods up the trail.

Well, we all thought, *at least Jim knows what he's doing.*

A young Sherpa emerged from the stone building carrying a plastic tray on which several worn menus were stacked. "*Namaste,*" he said, handing the menus to us.

We ordered bottles of Coke and yak cheeseburgers. He nodded and returned to the building. Ten minutes later, he brought Cokes and bottles of ketchup, encrusted around the caps. Twenty minutes later, still no yak cheeseburgers. Finally, a half hour later, he appeared again, with the cheeseburgers perched lopsidely on a plate. He smiled and placed them on the table in front of us.

I bit into my cheeseburger. It was well done, but delicious; it had a sharp, smoky flavor. I took a swig of Coke and another bite. I basked in the sun, the fresh air, the magnificent view of the mountains, new friends, and a cheeseburger. Life couldn't be better.

When we were full, we pushed back the stools and gathered up our gear. Since we were already dressed in our hiking clothes, we were ready to go. In our daypacks we each carried a map, compass, snack food, water bottles, headlamp, matches with candle, pocketknife, extra clothing, toothbrush, soap, and first-aid kit, along with passport, money, and camera gear. We would never let our daypacks out of sight. The duffels, carried by yaks, held the rest of our clothes, sleeping bags, books, extra food, and technical-climbing equipment.

We walked up the hill. Our yaks had already moved on ahead, prodded by their driver, Jettha (Jed-ah). In late afternoon, we crossed the airstrip, walked through the tiny village of Lukla among chickens, villagers, other trekkers, tea houses, and shops selling chocolate, postcards, sweaters, and jewelry, and found ourselves in the countryside in the soft late-afternoon light. We passed our first *mani* (mah-nee) wall, a long, low pile of flat rocks with prayers to Buddha carved into each stone. We would always pass to the left of a *mani* wall, out of respect to Buddha. The yaks would be driven to the left as well. On a narrow trail, this not only paid respect to Buddha, it also prevented traffic jams with yak trains traveling in different directions. We headed down the trail toward Phak Ding (Pahk Ding), where we would spend the night. We would be walking downhill most of this first day, from 9,200 feet to about 8,700 feet above sea level. The expedition had begun.

Soft peach, pink, and purple afterglow eased across the distant peaks. Kwangde rose to our left, behind the evergreen trees. Below

Jim and George pass to the left of a Buddhist mani wall. In the background, a string of prayer flags flutters in the breeze.

us, the Dudh Kosi (Dood Ko-see), "milky river," rushed south-west. Gradually, light left the mountains, the sky, the trail. We stopped to put on headlamps, sitting quietly on benches and rocks near the trail. Then we pressed on, picking our way over smooth boulders that lay in the middle of the trail as if we were nearly blind.

As I walked, I could hear the river roiling gently near me. Then I thumped down over a hollow bridge and into a dirt yard. We were at Phak Ding. In the dark, I could hear the snuffling and wandering of yaks. I could make out the dim shapes of another group's tents. Ahead, candlelight flickered through the windows of a low, wooden building, and we headed toward it.

Inside the room lay faded woven rugs and short sleeping benches with thick, heavy blankets worn smooth with dirt and grease. A long table, like a picnic table, stood at the center of the room. A cooking fire glowed in one corner and the air was pungent with smoke. Tin plates of food and plastic cups were laid before us, and we wolfed down dinner in semidarkness. Then we felt our way outdoors to our tents, where we slept peacefully among the wandering yaks.

In the morning, Dawa (Dah-wah), one of the Sherpas working with our trip, appeared at our tent door. "Tea!" he called softly, reaching in with a steaming pot and two plastic cups. I sat up in my sleeping bag and accepted the tea diluted with *dudh* (dood), or warm milk. Then Dawa placed two tin bowls of steaming water outside the tent. This was our washwater for the day. Hunched over, cross-legged, I pushed up my sleeves, drew my toothbrush out of my kit, and brushed my teeth. Then I splashed my face with warm water, droplets plunking in the dust outside the tent. I soaped up and rinsed my face, then dug out my nails with a nail file. This was as clean as I'd get for weeks.

We pushed our gear back into our daypacks and went to the lodge. We crowded into the small room for porridge, toast, and more tea. Then Jim introduced our Sherpa staff to us. Anu (Ah-noo) Sherpa was our *sirdar,* or the leader of the Sherpas on the trip. (All Sherpa people have the last name *Sherpa,* whether or not they belong to the same family.) Anu lived in Namche (Nam-chay) Bazaar, the busy trading village that we would trek to that day. Pasang (Pah-sahng) was our cook and the boss of the kitchen boys who worked for him. "Pasang" means "born on Friday." Jettha was the yak driver. Dendi (Den-dee), Kancha (Kahn-chah), and Nima (Nee-mah) were Sherpa guides who would later climb Island Peak with us, along with Anu. Dawa, Kami (Kah-mee), Purba (Per-bah), and Zangbu (Zang-boo) were the kitchen boys. "*Namaste*," they said to us. "*Namaste*," we answered.

Outside, after breakfast, Anu took charge. The yaks were rounded up and caught, and the large duffels anchored to wooden frames on their backs with thick, frayed rope. Dendi and Kancha swiftly struck camp and looped the tents onto the backs of more yaks. Then with a sharp whistle and a wave of his stick, Jettha moved them out of camp. The strong yaks lumbered along, swaying back and forth underneath their loads.

We hoisted our daypacks onto our shoulders and started up the trail in cool morning light. We would climb and drop to the river many times, gaining and losing a total of more than seven thousand feet in elevation. Our knees would ache and our lungs would burn. We would groan in frustration, rising and falling, rising and falling. But this day would begin our final conditioning.

The yaks wove a long, steady train, curving slowly up and down the trail. They grunted and swayed, the ropes creaking. Jettha whistled a high bird whistle, whipping his stick through the air.

As we followed the river, Anu explained a tragedy of the year before. Way up the Khumbu valley, rock and ice fell into a glacial lake; the lake overflowed and the river surged down the valley, destroying homes and carrying people away. "Many people die. *Whoosh!* Down the river," explained Anu. The surge also wiped out a power project designed to bring electricity to the lower valley.

We stopped to rest on the cool, pebbly beach next to the river. Scattered along the riverside, we lazed in the sun while Pasang and the kitchen boys prepared scrambled eggs, tuna, and breadlike *chappattis* for lunch. Purba came around with a pot of a sweet, warm orange-colored drink called squash. Jim typed messages on the tiny portable typewriter that he carried everywhere. George perched on a large boulder with a cup of squash while Jerry and Linda discussed camera gear. Boyd cleaned yak manure out of his boot with a stick. Shadows slid across the river toward my rock as I ate my eggs and tuna and sipped hot tea.

After lunch, we crossed the river and trudged up the steep, dusty trail toward Namche Bazaar, gaining about a thousand feet in elevation in forty-five minutes. My calves and shoulders ached. At a bend in the switchback, we turned a corner: Everest stood in the distance, a slim flag of cloud flying from the summit.

At the Everest Tea Shop—a platform tent hung over the river gorge—a small boy appeared and Anu introduced him to me as his eight-year-old son, Nima Tsering, (Nee-mah Sare-ing), who had come down the trail to greet us. Nima's dark, round face shone beneath his crew cut. He trotted up the trail and looked back at me, grinning. "Namaste," I called to him. He put his hands together in prayer position and answered, "Namaste." Then he took off again. I followed him, feeling tired but strong. He stopped and sat on a rock to wait for me, then trotted on. We walked together that way to his house in Namche, arriving at 3:30 in the afternoon.

Nima showed me the way up the narrow, dark stairs to a large room with a table and sleeping benches. We would eat dinner here, then sleep in our tents in the dirt courtyard out back. Gradually, everyone arrived and dusk gathered in the room. Anu's wife, Ang Lamu (Ahng Lah-moo), appeared at the doorway, her black tunic brushing the floor as she entered the room. "Namaste," she greeted us, offering a warm smile. A bare bulb hanging from the ceiling in the center of the room flicked on.

Electricity had only come to Namche Bazaar within the past couple of years. Lights, powered by a single generator that sat outside of town, came on at sunset and shut off at 10:00 P.M., so the whole town was thrown into light or darkness at once. People paid a tiny amount for the use of each socket and bulb.

We sat in the odd glow and ate a dinner of *momos* (special pastries filled with cheese or yak meat) along with cooked vegetables and rice. I began to feel the sharp bite of an itch at the back of my neck. I scratched it, and the feeling spread. Within minutes, a rash had traveled up my skull and down to my ankles.

Bugbites, I thought. I must have been bitten without realizing it. I took some medicine to try to get rid of the itch.

Then I didn't have time to think about it. Jim produced a rope and strung it over the doorjamb. We each hung from the rope with one hand to test our ascenders called jumars, one of the climbing tools we would need on Island Peak. Then Jim timed us as we put on our crampons, strapping them as quickly as possible. After that, we chose climbing helmets, trying them on and trading them until we each had one that fit. We checked our climbing boots and harnesses to make sure they were in good repair. Then we stashed all the climbing gear in one duffel bag, where it would be carried by a yak. We would not see it again until the day before we reached Island Peak.

MOUNTAIN METHODS

The Right Stuff:
What to Take on Your
Mountaineering Trip

Mountain climbing requires some special equipment. What you need depends on several things: whether you are hiking for the day or camping overnight; the season of the year; and whether your climb is technical (with rope) or nontechnical (without rope). You want good, sturdy equipment that will last; you don't need the latest craze in gear. You don't have to buy all of your equipment new, and you don't need to buy everything at once.

Order a few catalogs from outfitters and read them, comparing descriptions and prices. (For some names and addresses, see "Getting Started.") Talk with friends who climb and salespeople at outdoor shops, but make your own decisions about what to buy.

1. *Ten essentials.* No matter when or where you climb, there are ten essentials that you should always carry with you: map, compass, emergency food, filled water bottle, flashlight or headlamp with extra batteries, matches and candle, pocketknife, extra clothing, sunglasses or goggles, and first-aid kit. (See "Just in Case.")

2. *Gear for day hiking.* In addition to the ten essentials, you'll need the following items in your daypack: toilet paper, food (see "Mountain Methods: What to Eat on Your Mountaineering Trip"), litter bag, and watch.

3. *Gear for backpacking (overnight).* When you plan to sleep overnight, you'll need the following in your large backpack: tent or tarp, ground cloth, rain cover

for pack, sleeping pad, winter or summer sleeping bag in a stuff-sack, backpacking stove and fuel, cooking kit and utensils, water purifier, bag for hanging food, nylon cord for hanging wet clothes to dry, soap, toothbrush, and any medicine you require.

4. *Special gear for winter.* In winter, you may need snowshoes, crampons, an ice ax, and insulated water bottles.

5. *Gear for technical climbing.* You'll learn how to use these items in a technical-climbing course: helmet, rope, harness, slings, carabiners, ascenders and descenders, belay devices, ice ax, crampons, ice screws (for ice), and nuts and chocks (for rock).

4

Namche Bazaar:
A Busy Trading Village

JERRY, LINDA, and Allen decided to sleep indoors at Anu's house, stretched out head to foot along the narrow sleeping benches under the windows. The rest of us felt our way down the worn wooden stairway, out into the dirt lane, and along a wall to the door leading into Anu's backyard. Dendi and Kancha had set up our tents and their flaps fluttered softly in the breeze. Saying goodnight, Boyd and I crawled into our tent.

Our two duffels lay like giant sausages on either side of the tent; there wasn't much room in between. I turned around, facing the outside of the tent, and unlaced my boots, pushing them off my feet. We kept our boots out of the tent, just under the fly (outer covering), to minimize the amount of dirt spread around inside. I unrolled my sleeping bag and settled it on its pad. I slipped off my sweater and pushed the sleeves of my scratchy polypropylene shirt up my forearms. Then I rustled around in my daypack for my headlamp, found it, and adjusted it on my forehead. A blurred circle of light fell over my sleeping bag, and I reached for a book I had been reading. I didn't read long. The distant yapping of tiny dogs, the steady clanging of yak bells, and dim voices lulled me toward sleep. Then the lights of Namche went out, and so did I.

Outside in the dark, I heard the scuffling of feet and the zipper on our tent flap flew up.

"Tea," whispered Purba, clanking the pot against the ground. He handed in two scratched plastic cups filled with a blend of tea and milk. It couldn't be morning. My muscles ached from the long pull from Phak Ding to Namche the day before, and I felt as though I hadn't slept. I let the warm tea flow through me and fought the temptation to lie back down in my sleeping bag. Then the basins of washwater arrived, and I brushed my teeth, sloshed my face with water, pulled on my sweater and parka, shoved my feet into slightly damp hiking boots, and crawled out of the tent.

As I bent to tie my laces, blood rushed to my head. Boyd, right behind me, saw me sway and caught me.

"Is the altitude bothering you?" he asked.

"No," I answered. "I just feel as though I haven't slept." In the cold, blue light before dawn, the door to the courtyard creaked open and Jim entered the yard.

"Ready?" he called softly. I reached into the tent, pulled out my daypack and camera, then dragged out Boyd's, handing them to him. We joined Jim and the others in the street.

We were climbing the hill above Namche to watch the sunrise on Everest. We marched single-file, silently, and within minutes had left town. The trail angled sharply up the hill. Soon I was breathing hard. Namche Bazaar lies 11,300 feet above sea level, and we needed to acclimatize. Thus, we would spend a day here hiking in the area before moving on to higher altitudes. Working hard, I sweated in my too-heavy parka while cold air seared my lungs and my eyes grew puffy. My boots crunched over nearly frozen ground that would be a whirl of hot dust by midday. We switchbacked (zigzagged back and forth) up the hill while Namche slept below. I began to worry. I knew I was in good condition, and yesterday I had felt strong. But this morning I felt like a rag doll. My lungs were stretched to the limit, and I had no strength in my legs. While I was worrying, we reached the top of the hill.

"The sun will reach those mountains first," said Jim, pointing to Thamserku (Tahm-sare-koo) and Kwangde. "Then it will come around to Everest." We readied our camera gear in near darkness, bare fingers fumbling with the cold metal, and waited. Without warning, a pink patch of light touched a corner of Thamserku; then came a widening strip, then an acre of glorious pink. Mt. Everest, far across the valley, stood like a dark hunk of coal. Then the light touched the long plume of cloud streaming from the summit and ignited it, the fire of dawn spreading across Nuptse, Lhotse, and Everest. As the sun rose, we could see Tengboche (Teng-bo-shay), the Buddhist monastery perched on a ridge below Everest, to which we would hike the next day. In full morning light, we headed back to Namche.

Hungry for breakfast, we clomped into Anu's house. Pasang produced granola cereal, oily omelets and fried potatoes, thick toast with marmalade and peanut butter, and cup after cup of tea. With an open clay hearth for cooking and warmth, Anu's kitchen was a separate room across the hall from the main room. All along the trail, Pasang would use the ovens of friends or people who ran tea houses or guest houses.

"Since today is an acclimatization day, for your bodies to get used to the altitude, we'll stay here in Namche. You can go to the bazaar," suggested Jim. Once a week, an entire corner of Namche becomes the famous bazaar, in which Sherpas from all over the Khumbu come to buy and sell or trade their goods. Many Sherpas are farmers, growing potatoes, barley, buckwheat, and tea. They must travel a day or two to Namche, driving their yaks with heavy loads of crops to the bazaar. Other Sherpas are merchants or traders, buying and selling clothing and tools for cash. The average person in Nepal earns only about $160 per year. Until foreigners began to trek and climb in the Khumbu, hiring Sherpas to work on the expeditions, most earned far less than that. They simply lived on what they could farm.

George and Allen decided to hike outside the village. Linda was not feeling well and stayed indoors to rest. Jerry, Jim, Boyd, and I, laden with cameras, hurried down to the bazaar. We clambered up on a ledge above the market area to watch. Below us lay a monsoon of people. A colorful cloud of tunics, sweaters, caps, shawls, and scarves swarmed over goods we could hardly see: huge sacks of grain, boxes of vegetables and fruit, battered cans of fuel, bloody meat. Two young monks, wrapped in dull brown robes with maroon caps perched on their heads, crouched near us, watching the scene quietly from above. Two boys wandered up to me from behind, staring intently at my camera. They watched my movements without a word. When I pointed to them and back to the camera, they nodded, curious. I stood back and focused. They froze, their faces somber. Most Nepalese wear a serious expression in photographs. As warm and friendly as they are, a photograph is a solemn occasion. Many older people do not like their pictures taken. Some mothers even shield their children from the camera; they believe that the camera may capture their souls and their children's too. But by asking permission or taking pictures from far away, we avoided upsetting anyone.

We wandered down to the end of the market, where the butcher was located. (Although Sherpas do not kill animals themselves, they do eat meat. Members of other tribes are employed as butchers.) Jimmy motioned toward an old man with long braids and a thin veil of a beard that grew to a point just above his waist.

"Watch him," said Jimmy. "He's in the middle of a deal." The man pointed to the neck of an animal and gestured. He rocked from side to side in his worn hiking boots and down ski pants, adjusting an old cloth sack slung over his shoulder. The butcher laughed and waved him away, shaking his head. Scowling, the old man backed away, pushing into the crowd. He wandered from merchant to merchant, then made his way back to the butcher. He shouted again, a higher price. The butcher shook his head again, still laughing. Everyone around laughed, and the old man walked away again. Then he came back a third time, and tapped the butcher on the shoulder. The butcher gave a slight nod. The deal was closed. The old man reached into the grimy folds of his shirt and drew out a few rumpled rupees. Carefully, he counted them out, placing them in the hand of the butcher, mumbling. Then he crumpled the rest and stashed them back in his shirt. He bent over and dragged the neck away.

Pasang bought groceries at the bazaar, walking from merchant to merchant. He bought fresh eggs, a hunk of yak meat, potatoes, cheese, rice, vegetables, flour, and tea. We would eat a combination of Nepalese and American food on the trip. Some food would be canned, and the rest Pasang would buy along the trail, purchasing what he could. Once, be bought a chicken from a friend and we had chicken and rice. Pasang claimed to have a great deal of experience as a cook, but we had our doubts. Often he would stop friends along the trail, asking them for recipes. Whatever they told him appeared on our plates that night.

In addition to the food Pasang cooked, we ate high-energy snack food carried in our day packs: trail mix, dried fruit, and candy.

Boyd and I left the bazaar late in the morning and walked up to the Khumbu Lodge because we had heard that P.K. and his wife, the owners of the lodge, served enormous cinnamon rolls with tea. We pushed open the worm-eaten door and climbed a dark, musty staircase to the top, where a woman was bent over a large pot on an open fire.

"Cinnamon rolls?" I asked.

"Wait here," she replied, pointing to a room off the hallway. We wandered around the room, dust from our hiking boots rising in the sunlight. Photographs of former president Jimmy Carter lined the walls. President Carter had trekked through the Khumbu exactly a year before, climbing Kala Pattar (Kah-lah Pah-tahr), which we would do in a week or so. He had stayed at the Khumbu Lodge.

The woman shuffled in, carrying a plastic tray with glasses of tea thick with *dudh,* plus two huge cinnamon rolls. Carefully, she placed the glasses of tea, then the rolls, on a table carved with graffiti.

She saw me looking at the photos. "You know Jimmy Carter?" she asked.

"No, not personally," I answered. "He was our president from 1977 to 1981." Later we discovered that everywhere we hiked in the Khumbu, people asked us if we knew him. Apparently, they loved him.

After a lunch of hot beans, fried potatoes, toast, boiled eggs, cheese, steamed cauliflower, and tea at Anu's house, Nima invited us to hike with him to his home in the hills outside Namche Bazaar. Then, if we wanted, we could hike on to the Khumjung (Koom-jung) school and Khunde (Koon-day) hospital, both built by Sir Edmund Hillary.

Jimmy, Jerry; Boyd, and I followed Nima as he wound through the dusty streets of Namche Bazaar, past the one-room bank, trekking shops, tea shops, and lodges, up the steep hill, zigzagging among the stone houses, over the hard gray ground worn down by the hooves of yaks. Near the top of the hill, a white fence marked off a large area.

"What is that for?" Boyd asked Nima.

"The yaks eat too much," explained Nima. "The hill is falling away." The fence kept yaks away from the crumbling hill.

I turned and looked back. The village lay directly below, prayer flags flying and flat stone roofs baking in the sun. We crossed the Shyangboche (Shang-bo-shay) airstrip, a high-altitude runway designed to bring trekkers and visitors to the area. It is now closed because often when people stepped out of the planes they would collapse with the sudden change in altitude. Flying may be convenient and fast, but it doesn't give the body a chance to get used to its new environment.

From the front yard of Nima's low stone house, high on the hill, we could see Everest, Ama Dablam (Ah-mah Dah-blahm),

Namche Bazaar, the Sherpa trading village built into the side of a hill at 11,300 feet above sea level.

Thamserku, and Khumbila. Outside the house stood a tall pole lined with prayer flags, carrying their messages to Buddha on the breeze. Nima's wife leaned out of the window and waved, inviting us in to tea. Padding across the soft woodchips where the animals lived, we followed Nima into the house and climbed the narrow, oily staircase to the kitchen on the second floor of his home. Nima's wife, a beautiful woman wearing an old rust-colored cardigan sweater over her black tunic, heated water for tea over the fire. Nima went to the next room and got the best mugs for us. Three of his children clustered around his knees, glancing shyly at us, then quickly away. Nima's oldest daughter arrived with a basket of dried yak chips, which her mother threw on the fire for fuel. (The Sherpas dry the round, flat manure of yaks against a rock or the side of the house, then use the "chips" for fuel.) The stove was made of clay, like the adobe of American Indians. We were served steaming tea while Lhakpa, Nima's eight-year-old son, sat next to me, staring.

Nima showed us his sack of purchases from the bazaar that morning.

"Yo ke ho?" I asked, pointing to one package.

"Pabsa," he answered. (It was pasta.)

Boyd leaned back, bird-whistled for the children, then imitated all the animals in a barnyard. Everyone laughed. Lhakpa and his brother imitated Boyd, but Lhakpa was missing a front tooth and could only make a hissing sound. Nima moved to the fire and squatted contentedly by his wife, peeling roasted potatoes, which he ate with greasy fingers. The quick, musical mumble of Sherpa language flew back and forth between Nima and his wife.

Then Lhakpa asked his father if he could walk with us to Khumjung and Khunde. He would earn his way by carrying my pack. We all laughed. My pack was as big as Lhakpa. So Lhakpa came anyway, and I carried my own pack.

We thanked Nima's wife for tea and set out across the hill to Khumjung. Khumjung is the home of the first school to be built in the Khumbu region. Before 1961, there were no schools in the Himalaya of Nepal. Children worked the small plots of land owned by their parents, helped herd yaks, and did household chores. After Edmund Hillary climbed Mt. Everest with his Sherpa partner Tenzing Norgay in 1953, he wished to repay the great debt he felt he owed the Sherpas for all their help while he was climbing the mountain. When he asked what he could do, one old man said, "Our children have eyes, yet they do not see." The old man meant that the Sherpa children could not read.

So Hillary set about building a school for the Sherpas. This was difficult because many of the materials had to be carried a great distance; some even had to come all the way up the valley from Kathmandu, a two-week walk. But with help from his New Zealand friends and his Sherpa friends, Hillary built the school and hired a teacher. The school at Khumjung was such a success that members of other villages asked him to build schools for them, and gradually he built several in the area. Hillary still returns often to the Khumbu, helping the Sherpas build, farm, and improve their villages.

The tin roofs of the two school buildings flashed in the sun. School would let out in less than an hour. Classes are lively and noisy and students are eager to learn, but there aren't many supplies. Teachers use a combination of textbooks, magazines, and whatever else is available to teach their students reading, writing, arithmetic, history, and geography.

As we passed the school, I began to feel tired and weak. I couldn't figure out why. I was eating enough food and drinking enough water. I was no longer breathing hard in the thin air. But the medicine I had taken to relieve the itching of the day before had left me groggy, and I had begun to feel the itching again, around my ankles and neck.

"Go on ahead to the hospital," I said to the others. "I'm going to rest here and then walk back to Namche." So Nima, Jerry, Lhakpa, and Boyd headed for Khunde, where they would tour the two-room hospital built by Hillary.

I sat on a rock for a while, soaking in the sun. I tore off the wrapper of a fruit bar and spun open the top of my water bottle. Maybe I'd have more energy if I had more fuel.

Then I walked down the pale green hill. Clumps of grass clung to dry earth where yaks had overgrazed. I arrived back in the cool, damp main room of Anu's house in late afternoon. Linda was there, pale and gloomy, her legs tucked up under her wool skirt.

"Why not go for a walk in the sun?" I suggested.

"Because I'm cold, and I don't want to get colder," she said. Actually, it was colder in Anu's house than it was outside. But Linda wasn't feeling well and was sinking into depression. She didn't want to accept suggestions that might help her feel more comfortable. A foreign country such as Nepal can seem strange and overwhelming because of the language, the culture, the lack of comfort, and the altitude. Jerry and Linda had climbed Mt. Kilimanjaro in Africa, but they didn't do any regular camping or climbing at home, so they weren't used to living outdoors. Now Linda was paying for it.

I stretched out on one of the sleeping benches. Above the east row of windows hung portraits of the king and queen of Nepal.

Every family in Nepal who can afford these portraits has them hanging in the home; today the pictures were especially important because it was the queen's birthday. In Anu's backyard, the town held a ceremony honoring the queen's birthday, complete with local officials, banners, speeches, and music. The wealthy king and queen are respected by even the poorest people in Nepal.

The rest of the walls in the main room held posters of various mountaineering expeditions and two goat carcasses drying out. One carcass had a pair of binoculars hanging around its neck. Except for the one light bulb, there was nothing else electric in the house—no stove, no refrigerator, no computer, no hair dryer, no stereo, no TV. In fact, television had just reached Nepal in 1986 and was still available only in Kathmandu for a few hours a day.

Anu stuck his head through the door. "*Namaste!*" he said, then looked at Linda with concern. "You are not well," he observed and offered to bring her a cup of tea.

Anu was in his midforties. He had had only one year of formal schooling, yet he spoke five languages: Tibetan, Sherpa, Nepali, English, and Japanese. Anu came to Nepal before the Chinese invaded Tibet. When the Sherpas began to flee Tibet, Anu had a government job much like an immigration officer. He kept close watch on the people who came to Nepal from Tibet, looking for those who came illegally. "But I didn't like working against my people this way," he told me, "so I left that job."

During the late 1960's and early 1970's, Anu worked on foreign-government projects, including laying pipeline in western Nepal. He also began to porter (carry loads) for expeditions. At first, he worked for Japanese expeditions, including a special photography trek. Later, he worked for several major climbing expeditions. Anu had been to Kathmandu. He had even been to Europe— to Switzerland to visit a wealthy client. Anu was very unusual among his friends; many Sherpas never even see Kathmandu.

Anu had several children. The oldest son, age fourteen, studied medicine in Kathmandu. The middle son, age nine, wanted to be a monk.

"Why?" I asked.

"He doesn't like girls," answered Anu. "When he hears his friends speak of the wife, he does not want to be married."

I laughed. "My brothers didn't like girls either. Now they are married."

"Ang Lamu would like him to be a monk," explained Anu. "He would live in Tengboche, which is not far away." The youngest boy, Nima Tsering, will take care of his parents when he grows up. In many Sherpa families, the oldest son gets a job to make money for the family; the middle son or daughter becomes a monk or nun; and the youngest takes care of the parents when they grow old.

At dinnertime, everyone drifted in and we attacked more fried potatoes, yellow with curry, huge mounds of sticky rice, and cooked vegetables. But I wasn't as hungry as I usually was after hiking; I was beginning to lose my appetite. And the rash was coming back. By now, huge welts covered my legs and arms and were spreading across my body. The itching had grown painful. I drew Jim aside and told him.

"I don't know what it is," he said. "I flagged down a couple of doctors today and asked their opinions. One said it might be the smoke from the cooking fires. Another said it might be the iodine in the water, or the anti-malaria pills we've all been taking. You're allergic to something, but we don't know what. Let's try to keep you out of these smoky buildings and stop purifying your water. I'll have Pasang boil extra water for you to drink. I think you can stop taking the anti-malaria pills. Malaria is carried by mosquitoes, and as we reach a higher altitude and colder climate, the mosquitoes will disappear."

I crept out to the tent with Boyd. A cloud of dust followed, sneaking inside and drifting into every fold of clothing, on the sleeping bag, even into my skin and mouth. Settling into the routine of living outdoors for a long period of time, no matter how much experience you have, can be tedious. Everything in the tent must be organized painstakingly, with each item in its place. When I crawled into the tent, debris lay everywhere: clothes, gear, camera equipment. I shoved it all aside and did my best to repack my duffel. I pulled off my sweater and pushed up the sleeves of my shirt. The welts were huge and rock hard. I say down, trying to forget about them. Then I began to feel my throat close, and welts traveled up to my face. I couldn't breathe.

I grabbed Boyd. Quickly he went for the medicine that might help. I swallowed two tablets with a gulp of water and waited. Within seconds, the swelling began to subside. I could breathe again.

"I'm scared," I confessed to Boyd.

He tried not to let his worry show. "We'll find you some help," he soothed. "We're going to figure this out."

Anger and fear pulsed through me. I hadn't come all this way to be knocked flat by a case of hives. But something was clearly wrong. I slid into my sleeping bag, listening to the yowling dogs, distant voices, and yaks ambling around the yard. I refused to let myself think about a hot bath, clean clothes, a tangy pizza, my favorite radio station—home.

MOUNTAIN METHODS

What to Eat on Your Mountaineering Trip

When you go mountain climbing, you need food that tastes good and gives you energy. You also want food that is light-weight, doesn't have to be refrigerated, and won't crumble or become crushed in your backpack. If you are camping and cooking, you want food that does not take long to prepare.

Foods that give high energy are carbohydrates (nuts, vegetables, fruits, sweets, and pasta); proteins (meat, fish, cheese, cereal, and nuts); and fats (nuts and sweets). You should eat a combination of all three, not just a lot of one.

Many outdoor-equipment stores sell freeze-dried packages of food, which are easy to prepare. But often you can find similar food at a lower cost at the supermarket.

Food for Day Trips

Take food that you don't need to cook. A bag of "gorp" or trail mix—made of nuts, raisins, other dried fruit (such as apples, apricots, or bananas), sunflower or soy seeds, and candy—provides you with energy from all three groups of food. A fresh apple or orange, as well as dried meat (salami, beef jerky, or pepperoni), can be sliced with your pocketknife. Firm cheese, such as cheddar or Monterey jack, will last for a day in your pack. Round, flat pita bread will not get squashed in your pack. You can take peanut butter in a squeeze tube (which you can buy at an outdoor shop).

Food for Overnight Trips

Plan all of your meals ahead of time. You can eat the same food for lunch that you eat on day trips, but you need to plan breakfasts and dinners. In addition to drinking water, you need water for cooking and washing pots. Remember that if you are camping above five thousand feet elevation, water will take longer to boil.

Breakfast: Hot instant oatmeal is especially good in winter. Fresh fruit or a Pop-Tart is good in summer. Hot tea or decaffeinated coffee is fine, but caffeine dehydrates you. Powdered milk and juice drinks are good.

Dinner: Stick with one-pot meals. Powdered soup, with an onion or carrot thrown in, is a great starter. Rice, packaged macaroni and cheese, and canned chicken or tuna can be eaten separately or cooked together. Instant pudding makes a good dessert.

5
A Buddhist Monastery

SOUNDS OF THE VILLAGE drew me toward waking. Dawa brought tea and washwater, and groggily I went through the motions of morning. At breakfast inside Anu's house, we discussed our next destination.

"First we'll climb the hill outside Namche and visit the Sherpa museum," said Jim. "You'll see exhibits about Sherpa life. Then we'll head toward Tengboche, the Buddhist monastery. Tonight, we'll camp beyond the monastery in the yard of a convent called Deboche" (Deh-bo-chay).

Pasang passed around a bowl of hard-boiled eggs. I took one and broke the shell, peeling it off in chips. I bit into the soft, rubbery egg. I wasn't very hungry and my stomach was unsettled. I reached into my pocket and took out an antacid tablet, washing it down with lukewarm tea.

The sun was already strong, and I had decided to climb in cotton pants and my polypropylene shirt, with my wool trekking sweater knotted around my waist. I had taped my heels the day before to prevent blisters and now wore one pair of thin socks and one pair of thick cotton socks inside my hiking boots. In my daypack, I carried raingear and a windbreaker along with a heavier jacket, gloves, and a wool hat in case it got cold later. Today we would start hiking at 11,300 feet and wind up at about 12,700 feet, in Tengboche. Chances were, it would be a lot colder up there so I wanted my heavier clothes nearby.

By the time we finished breakfast, Dendi and Kancha had dropped the tents to the ground and were rolling them tight. Nima had spent the night with his family up on the hill and would join us on the trail. In a steady stream, we marched up the side of the hill, leaving the bustle of Namche Bazaar far below. Although we would pass through other small settlements and villages, Namche was the last major town we would see for several weeks. We were now headed further into the wilderness, higher into the mountains.

Hikers equipped for spring, summer, or fall climbing carry their backpacks high up on their shoulders and wear layers of clothing.

Jettha veered off on the trail directly toward Tengboche, winding the yaks up and down the path that clung to the hill. The rest of us climbed to the museum while Jim stopped at a special government checkpoint to have our trekking and climbing permits stamped. When trekking and climbing in Nepal, you must get a permit from the government that states where you are going. Everest is actually in a national park—called Sagarmatha National Park—that has checkpoints where all climbers and trekkers must stop.

Inside the museum, we learned about the economy, religion, and customs of the Sherpas. We saw exhibits of tools that they use and clothes that they wear. We saw pictures of weddings and holiday festivals.

Midmorning, we stepped back out into the sunlight and walked toward the main trail leading to Tengboche. We clomped along as the milky blue Dudh Kosi raged a thousand feet below. High above us, on the left, a shaggy brown tahr—a goat—grazed on the brown hill. A huge, black lammergeier, like a large hawk, reeled over the gorge. Feeling warm, I pushed the sleeves of my shirt up over my elbows. Boyd shed his red windbreaker. The others peeled off layers as well, feeling the heat build up as they worked hard in the sun.

Straight ahead stood Ama Dablam, 22,350 above sea level, which the Nepalese call the most beautiful mountain in the world. Its name means "mother's charmbox," referring to the square ornament a Sherpa woman wears around her neck. The square, icy summit of Ama Dablam looked like a charmbox. Its wide snowfields gleamed, the long arms of its ridges reaching out on either side. In the distance, Everest beckoned us. Tengboche rested on a ridge below the massive peaks, the long thread of trail angling up through bare trees to the low buildings. We swung along, feeling that we wanted to be nowhere else in the world.

By late morning, the trail dipped steeply to a stream. We stopped, unlaced our boots, and sank our feet into the freezing water. I lay back in the sun, suddenly feeling sleepy and weak. I ate a granola bar, crinkling the wrapper and stuffing it in my pocket. *I just want a nap,* I thought. *If I can sleep for twenty minutes, I'll be fine.* I closed my eyes.

I heard a voice. "Hi there," said Jim. He leapt across the stream. He had started out behind us and was now catching up. He squatted beside me. "How are you feeling?"

"OK," I answered. "Just a little tired."

"Have a snack for some energy," he suggested. "I don't think you should lie down for too long." I sat up, took a few bites of a fruit bar, had a drink of water, and stood. I felt a little better, but not great. I moved on as if I were walking in a dream.

We climbed again. Then the trail dropped to a small village with a tea house. Jim disappeared into the house and returned with several cloudy glasses of tea. We sat on a log outside the house and sipped the tea. At the side of the trail, a prayer wheel turned continuously, powered by water from the river. Trekkers and villagers passed by, greeting us with *"Namaste."* A girl sat on a blanket near the house, selling jewelry made of tin, coral, and turquoise. A few boys played a game in the dirt near her.

We finished our tea and returned the glasses to the house. Inside, behind a counter, the house was stocked like a general store with old chocolate bars, jars of dark, oily peanut butter made in India, and ancient tins of marmalade. On one shelf lay a few dusty post-cards and bars of soap. Outside, we shrugged our daypacks back onto our sore shoulders and started back up the trail.

Later, clouds began to roll in, surging up the valley. A chill soaked into my skin. Layer by layer, we dressed in our heavier clothes. I put on my sweater and hat. (I knew I would lose more than 80 percent of my body heat through my head.) Boyd put on his windbreaker, and Linda bundled up in a wool jacket. Jimmy wore his red and black checkered wool shirt. As we wound our way through the soft pine forest, I began to lose strength again. I knew the altitude wasn't bothering me, and I'd had enough to eat. As I fell behind, Nima took my pack. Deep purple clouds gathered around us, threatening snow.

As I walked, head down, pushing upward, I thought about mountaineering. I was sick, uncomfortable, and tired, but still I wanted to be here, in the Himalaya. I knew that whether or not I made it to the top of Island Peak, I would go as far as I could and do my best; and I knew that these mountains would stay with me, in my mind, for the rest of my life.

Mist curled around the hill, crawling up through the trees, enclosing the mountains inside it. The afternoon light grew flat and dull. We trudged on, up over the last knoll, passing to the left of the *chorten* (a stone shrine honoring Buddha), and stood at the entrance to Tengboche.

Monks in red or orange robes floated back and forth across the yard; yaks milled around, their bells clanging dimly through the fog; tiny black dogs yapped from the stairs leading to the main building. Jim and Nima directed us to a small tea house and we ducked into the smoky room.

Nima slipped off my pack and dropped it on the ground next to the door. We moved closer to the fire, pulling up benches toward the warmth. Nima disappeared and returned with several cups of tea.

"Thank you," I said, accepting the tea. I felt guilty, though. The tea must have cost him several rupees, a good part of his day's wages. But it would have been rude to refuse the tea or insist on paying for it.

Tengboche is a *gompa,* or Buddhist monastery, and is the major center of Buddhist life in the Khumbu, although there are other monasteries in the region. At Tengboche, men and boys study to become Buddhist monks; then they continue to live and work there. Tengboche has one head monk whose leadership the others follow. Although the people who live at the monastery are separate from the surrounding villages, they are considered to be a part of village life. The monks also welcome visitors. A Sherpa may choose to become a monk for several reasons. He may be an orphan who needs a home. He may be especially bright in literature and philosophy, and the monastery will give him the right atmosphere and encouragement in his study. Or he may be following his family's wishes. Although the monks at Tengboche live a simple life, they are usually comfortable.

Tengboche was founded in the 1920's. Although there were other Buddhist monasteries in existence in the Khumbu, Tengboche was the first to be organized and structured. Tengboche is also the site of many elaborate religious ceremonies in which both monks and villagers take part. In November, the people celebrate Mani Rimdu (Mah-nee Rim-doo), a holiday that lasts several days and includes many long dances and performances that depict the triumph of Buddhism over a more ancient faith. Anu's family sometimes attends the Mani Rimdu festival at Tengboche.

After our tea, we took up our packs and headed toward Deboche, feeling our way through dusk to the camp. Jimmy, Allen, and George sprinted ahead and were tossing *makai* (mah-kie)—popcorn—into their mouths, warming themselves in the meal tent, when the rest of us arrived. I wasn't hungry. I slid into the sleeping tent and Boyd followed.

I unrolled my sleeping bag and stretched out. In minutes, the hives began to travel up my legs, arms, neck, throat, and head. My face went numb and hard, like a mask.

"Get Jim," I said to Boyd. "Fast." Boyd gave me some medicine before leaving the tent. When he was gone I lay there alone, trying not to be frightened. Gradually, the numbness subsided and breathing was easier. But my upper lip still had no feeling. I could hear Jim and Boyd talking in low voices outside the tent. Then Jim stuck his head in and asked me some questions. Boyd volunteered to bring me a plate of dinner from the meal tent. I felt drained, but I just wasn't hungry. I crawled out of the tent and got sick. When Boyd returned with dinner, I tried to eat but got sick again, the burning liquid traveling from my stomach up into my mouth.

I knew that if I couldn't eat, I was in trouble. I would just get weaker and weaker. We were a long way from help: there was no doctor, no telephone, no ambulance. We had to help ourselves. Evacuation is almost impossible in Nepal. There are only two helicopters in the whole country, and both of them belong to the king and queen. The helicopters are only available for rescue operations if the king and queen are not using them for social or official engagements. Besides, contacting Kathmandu quickly requires having a two-way radio, but there was none in the area. I realized how important it is to be your own best resource for help in the mountains.

I tried to sit up to join the others in the meal tent, but I was too dizzy. Gradually, I fell asleep.

During the night, snow dusted the yard and the peaks above. In the morning, I pulled on an extra layer of clothes, drank my tea, washed up, and poked my head out of the tent. Cold morning light touched the peaks. I shuffled through the frost to the meal tent, where Jim and the group were discussing plans for the day.

"Today we'll have another rest day, since we are now at nearly thirteen thousand feet above sea level," Jim said. "If you want, you can hike for the day and see some of the local sights." He looked at me. "You should take the day to rest. Get your strength back. Tomorrow, you, Boyd, and I will try to hike to the Himalayan Rescue Association, where there will be some doctors. Jerry and Linda, today you must decide whether or not you want to continue the climb. I'd like to talk with you both after breakfast."

I was surprised by Jim's remark. I knew that Linda was unhappy, but I hadn't realized that she and Jerry were thinking of going home.

"Just wait," I said to Linda. "Things will get better. The higher up we go, the more beautiful it will be. You'll get used to it." Linda looked at me blankly. I was sick, and I was telling her that everything would be fine. She didn't believe me. I glanced around the tent. We were quite a crew: I was sick; Jerry and Linda were planning to go home; both Boyd and Allen were showing signs of a struggle with the altitude. This wasn't a very good start to the climb at all.

I spent the day reading and walking around the yard at Deboche, frustrated and angry, feeling my physical strength drain away. But I would not go home; I just couldn't. We had come too far. At lunch, Pasang served one of my favorite dishes, cheese *momos*. "I love these," I said, but only reached for one. Then I raced outside. I took an antacid to try to settle my stomach but got sick again.

After a restless night for me, we ate our last breakfast together. Then Kancha tied Jerry and Linda's gear to a yak and we shook hands all around.

"You should come with us," Linda said to me. I shook my head. We watched the three trekkers and their yak start back down the trail, slowly and deliberately. We were sorry to see them go, but we were relieved. They had made their own decision. Now we focused our sights on Island Peak.

MOUNTAIN METHODS

What to Wear on Your Mountaineering Trip

Dressing for mountain climbing is not a fashion show. You don't need to buy all new clothes. Find some in your closet, then buy any special items from an outdoor-equipment shop or outfitter's catalog. (For names and addresses, see "Getting Started" at the back of this book.)

When you are climbing, the most important job your clothes have is to keep you warm and dry. They should "breathe" (allow perspiration out while keeping body heat in). The trick to this is wearing layers. You may be cold when you start to hike, become hot while hiking, and suddenly cool down again when you stop. You should be able to remove and add layers as you need them. The right clothes can help you prevent two serious conditions: hypothermia and heat exhaustion.

Boots

When you climb in the mountains, your feet and ankles need support. There are many kinds of hiking boots. For most nontechnical climbing, light or medium-weight boots are fine. If you are climbing a snowy mountain, you may need plastic mountaineering boots. If you are learning technical rockclimbing, your instructor may ask you to wear rockclimbing shoes. Don't buy boots from a catalog. Go to the store. A good salesperson will ask you several questions about what kind of climbing you plan to do. Fit is the most important thing, so try on as many pairs of boots as you need to. Even after you buy your boots, wear them around the house before you go hiking. If they aren't comfortable, take them back.

Warm-Weather Clothes

You will need two pairs of socks (one thin, one thick); loose-fitting shorts or light-weight pants; short-sleeve shirt; long-sleeve shirt or sweater; windbreaker; rain gear; and hat (to protect you from sun and bugs).

Cold-Weather Clothes

You will need two pairs of socks (one thin, one thick wool); polypropylene or Capilene long underwear, top and bottom (polypropylene and Capilene are special fabrics that keep you from becoming damp and clammy); wool pants (not jeans, which get cold and wet quickly); wind pants if necessary; wool shirt or sweater; parka (wind- and water-resistant); wool hat; both mittens and gloves; scarf or face mask; and gaiters (leg coverings) for snow.

6
Ngorup: A Sherpa Boy

JIM TOLD ME, "You can ride a yak if you want." The thought made my stomach lurch.

"No, thank you," I replied. "I can walk." As rotten as I felt, the idea of sloshing around on the back of a yak seemed much worse than walking. But I gave my pack to Mingma, a young Sherpani (Sherpa woman) who was working with us for a couple of days. When I dragged the pack from my tent after breakfast, it felt as though it weighed a hundred pounds.

We began the day's journey. George, Jimmy, and Allen took off fast. Up the trail, they would veer off toward Dingboche (Ding-bo-chay), the yak-herding camp that was our next planned stop. Boyd, Jim, and I would head in a slightly different direction, toward Pheriche (Fair-i-chay), a small village where the Himalayan Rescue Association was located. There, we hoped to find doctors who could help me.

To pass the time as we walked, Jim told the story of Ngorup (Neh-rup) Yondon Sherpa and how their lives had come together. In the fall, not long after he had moved to Kathmandu from America to become a mountain guide in the Himalaya, Jim had led a trekking trip into the Khumbu.

Along the trail, a man and a woman who were members of the trip asked him, "Are there any orphanages up here in the Khumbu?"

"I don't know of any," said Jim. "But there are a lot of orphanages down in Kathmandu. Why?"

"We think we might adopt a Nepalese child," said the husband.

Jim turned to the Sherpa *sirdar* who was on the trek and asked, "Are there any orphanages in the Khumbu?"

"No, no orphanages," answered the sirdar. "But some people have children they cannot keep."

Jim then said to the *sirdar,* "If you know of any person with such a child, let us know." The group continued its trek to Everest Base

Camp and after a couple of weeks returned to Lukla, where they would catch their plane back to Kathmandu. They thought no more about a child.

On the evening they reached Lukla, the group *sirdar* came to Jim and said, "The child is here. He can go down to Kathmandu and he's ready to go to America."

Jim was startled. "What?" He asked. "What do you mean, the child is here? Let me see." So he left the trekking group and followed the *sirdar* into the dusk. A few yards away stood a mother and child. Jim recognized the mother—she was a Sherpani who had worked for him as a porter on other treks. Her daughter, who stood close by, was about thirteen years old. Jim had especially noticed the two because they were a mother and daughter who worked as a team and because the girl was so young to be carrying such heavy loads along the trail. Nestled between the two was a small child, looking up at Jim and the *sirdar*. The mother rested her hand on his shoulder and gestured.

"Here he is," she said to Jim.

Jim replied, "We can't just take him. Adoption is more complicated than this." But the child was ready to go, and his mother was ready to send him. Jim tried to speak with the woman for a few minutes, but her main language was Sherpa, and she did not speak good Nepali. He walked over to her Sherpa interpreter and asked, "Are you sure that you want your boy to go to America?"

"Yes, I'm sure," she answered through the interpreter. "I'm very poor. You see me working on the trail as a porter, carrying loads. I have to give this boy up."

Jim went back to his group and found the couple who had thought they wanted to adopt a Nepalese child. "What do you think?" he asked them. They had discussed it during the trek and decided that they wanted to adopt a girl. In addition, they were afraid that if they took the Sherpa child to America, other children in their town might not accept the youngster because he looked so different from them. So they said no. At first, Jim was relieved because he did not want to get involved with a complicated international adoption.

So he reported to the *sirdar*, "They've changed their minds. You'll have to send the boy back to his home." He started to leave.

The *sirdar* was disappointed. He explained, "But they've walked all the way here from their village, Thami (Tah-mee). They have walked for two days."

Jim turned back. "Oh. I'll tell you what. I'll give you two hundred rupees—that's ten dollars. Give that to them, and it should cover their expenses. Send them back to the village. Tell them it's a mistake."

The *sirdar* returned to the woman, and Jim's trekking group settled into their tents at Lukla for their final evening. A few hours later, the *sirdar* came back to Jim and said, "Come with me for a minute, will you please?" He led the way to a small sleeping tent pitched in the dirt. He ducked inside, and Jim followed. Inside the small tent crouched two Buddhist monks. In the near dark, Jim recognized one of the monks as an important religious figure: the *rinpoche* (ran-po-shay). The *rinpoche* is believed to be reincarnated and thus is considered to be very wise. This monk was also the head lama, or leader, of the Thami *gompa* (monastery), from where the mother and child had come.

As the men exchanged greetings, Jim studied the *rinpoche*. He was a young man, about twenty-five—Jim's age. His face and eyes radiated a soft glow, even in the darkness of the tent. He looked very, very wise.

Sitting beside the *rinpoche* was another monk—the uncle of the child. He was the chief administrator of the Thami *gompa*; in other words, he was the *rinpoche*'s most important assistant. Jim sat cross-legged in the tent, hunched forward, with his elbows on his knees. He and the *sirdar* faced the two monks, separated by a sleeping pad that lay in the center of the tent.

Quietly, the child's mother, Lhakpa Dhiki (Lahk-pah Dee-kee), appeared, holding a jug from which she poured *chang,* the traditional country drink, into four small jelly jars. Each of the men took a drink, as was traditional and sociable.

One monk said, "It is too bad that the American couple has backed down from their offer to take the boy to America."

Jim nodded. "Yes, but he's probably better off in the Khumbu. In America, there are all kinds of problems, and people might not like him. Besides, there aren't any monasteries in America. He probably wouldn't be a Buddhist if he grows up in America."

The monks inclined their heads. "We understand," they said. "We know that you meant well." The men continued to talk, and Lhakpa Dhiki poured more *chang*.

The monks asked, "Isn't there something that you might do? The boy and his mother are very, very poor. They need help."

Jim shrugged his shoulders. "I don't see what I can do. I'm not married, and I don't have much money. I can't raise him alone." Jim began to realize that the *sirdar* was caught in the middle. He had made a promise to the boy and his mother as well as to the monks; and now he was in trouble. Worse, he had made an offer in front of the *rinpoche,* and now the offer was to go unfulfilled.

The *sirdar* turned to Jim. "I will bring the boy into my own house," he offered. "That would relieve his mother of the burden of feeding him and raising him. But if I have him in my house, would you pay for his school?"

Jim scanned the faces around the tent. "I don't know. How much does the school cost?" He learned that it was about fifteen dollars a month. Yes, he could pay that. Even if he left Nepal and returned to America, he could still send the boy his school money. So he agreed.

Jim then asked the *sirdar,* "Are you sure you can have him in your own house?"

The *sirdar* replied, "Oh, yes. I have four sons already. He will be the fifth son." So they agreed to the arrangement, and the monks approved happily.

Sometime during the discussion, the five-year-old boy had slipped into the tent and was sprawled on the floor among the men, gazing at them as if he knew they were deciding his whole future, right then and there.

When Jim woke up the next morning, he wasn't sure whether he had been dreaming. Was he to take responsibility for a Sherpa boy? Perhaps it was just one of those things that happens often in Nepal—something is talked about at great length, but never comes to pass.

He pushed thoughts of the situation from his mind. He gathered together the trekking group and their gear, and they waited in the dusty sun near the airstrip for the tiny plane that would take them back to Kathmandu. When the warning siren sounded, the plane buzzed in from the horizon, bounced up the runway, and skidded to a halt.

A crowd of villagers had gathered to greet the plane. From the throng Lhakpa Dhiki emerged, carrying the small child in her arms. He seemed even tinier than he had the night before, and frightened. As she held the boy out to Jim, Lhakpa Dhiki wept. Jim gathered Ngorup into his arms, feeling his tiny bones through his ragged shirt. Ngorup looked back at his mother and began to cry.

"Good luck down in the city, son!" the villagers shouted, their voices nearly drowned in the noise of the plane.

Not knowing what else to do, Jim started toward the plane with Ngorup in his arms, surrounded by the trekking group. He carried the small boy up the rickety stairs and into the dim light of the plane, adjusting the child on his lap like a rucksack. The plane revved its engine and Ngorup clung to Jim as it rolled down the runway, off the cliff, and into the air.

Half an hour later, the plane drifted down onto the runway in Kathmandu. Wide-eyed, Ngorup stared out the window. Jim carried him to the parking lot and set him down. Several taxis pulled up to take the group to town. Ngorup walked over to a cab and touched it gently with his hand, petting it as if it were a yak. He had seen planes before in Lukla, but he had never seen a car. Then the group piled into two small taxis and whipped through the streets of Kathmandu—past wandering cows and people on bicycles, dodging other cars—to the hotel where they were to stay.

In Jim's room at the hotel, Ngorup looked around at the huge bed, instead of mats on the floor; the bureau, instead of a small wooden trunk; the chairs, instead of benches. "Whose house is this?" he asked Jim. "Is this your house?"

"No," answered Jim. "This is called a hotel."

Ngorup went over to the window and stared at his almond-colored reflection in the glass. He touched the quills of his black hair and watched his reflection do the same. Then he pressed his palm against the cool glass. "What is this?" he asked.

"That is called glass," replied Jim.

The American group went home. The next day, Jim and Ngorup moved to the *sirdar's* house in Kathmandu, where they set up a large canvas dining tent in the yard in which to live. Only two of the *sirdar's* sons were at home, and his wife welcomed Ngorup, but Ngorup wanted to sleep in the tent with Jim.

Each day, Jim perched Ngorup on the back of his bicycle. Together they would bump and wobble through the streets of Kathmandu as Jim went to appointments and meetings. Ngorup roamed the shops and followed the wandering Hindu cows. He learned to leap out of the way of speeding cars. And he got used to the steady glare of electric lights instead of the gentle glow of candles.

This was the longest school vacation of the year, so Ngorup stayed with Jim every day for the next two months. One day, the *sirdar's* brother visited Jim. "We heard about this child," the man began. "You don't really understand the situation. This man, the *sirdar,* has a good heart, and he likes to promise things to people, but he has four children already and he can't afford another one. The boy will have to go back to the Khumbu."

Once Ngorup woke in the middle of the night, sick. He stumbled to the edge of the tent and vomited; then he crawled back to bed, where Jim gave him water to drink.

Shivering, Ngorup whimpered, "I want to go back to my mother."

Jim soothed him. "It's all right, you'll be going back to your mother soon."

But the next morning, Ngorup woke early and shook Jim awake. "I want to stay here," he said.

Jim began to worry. How could he care for the boy alone? Perhaps he could place Ngorup in boarding school, but still make certain that Ngorup would visit his mother in the Khumbu once a year. When he investigated the cost, he learned that boarding school was about fifty dollars a month—a lot of money, but he thought he could pay it.

Before making the final decision, however, Jim took Ngorup back to the Khumbu to visit his mother, Lhakpa Dhiki. When he found her, he explained, "Things aren't working out in Kathmandu. The family can't keep Ngorup." Lhakpa Dhiki appeared disappointed, but she didn't say anything. So Jim hired her to work as a porter on the trek he was leading, and along the trail he found an interpreter who spoke both Sherpa and English.

Through the interpreter he asked Lhakpa Dhiki, "Do you want to have Ngorup here or there?"

"I'd like to have him down in Kathmandu," responded Lhakpa Dhiki. "I want him to go to school."

Jim said, "He's been down there a month and now back here for a month. He's been without you and you without him. Are you sure you don't want to raise him yourself?"

Lhakpa Dhiki explained, "I have a plan for my family." She told Jim her story. When she was younger, Lhakpa Dhiki was a Buddhist nun, living in a nunnery. She had learned how to read Tibetan and she was very religious. Then she met a monk who had come from Tibet to the Thami *gompa;* he was not only a monk but also a Tibetan doctor. Lhakpa Dhiki and the monk fell in love. In Nepal and Tibet, it is not wrong or shameful for a monk and nun to fall in love and leave the order; in fact, the monastery gave them a house in which to live. Lhakpa Dhiki's husband was old for a Sherpa, probably in his early fifties. They had four children together, and then he died, several years later. At the time he died, Lhakpa Dhiki was only in her early thirties.

Lhakpa Dhiki was still very religious when Jim met her. She hoped to spend her older years praying and devoting herself to her religion. Of her four children, she wanted one boy to become a monk/doctor and one of the girls to become a nun. She needed the other girl to stay with her, to keep her and care for her when she grew old. In the Tibetan monasteries of Nepal, the monks and nuns must be supported; someone must send them money. Lhakpa Dhiki had no money or property, so she needed her fourth child— Ngorup—to become educated so that he could get a job down in the city and send her enough money to live on. She didn't expect him to have a prestigious job or one that paid a lot of money—just enough to support his brother and sister in the monasteries and to care for her as she grew older.

Jim listened carefully as Lhakpa Dhiki told her story. He had only known her under the weight of her portering loads, walking up and down the trail. He began to understand why it was so important to the family that Ngorup go to school: eventually, Ngorup would keep the whole family going. So Jim agreed to the plan. "He'll go to boarding school," he assured Lhakpa Dhiki. "I will send him the money."

At the end of the month, Jim took Ngorup back to Kathmandu, where he located a school and bought Ngorup the few clothes he needed—a school uniform and several shirts and pairs of pants.

Lhakpa Dhiki's plan began to come true. Her oldest daughter, Dolma, entered the nunnery. Her youngest daughter, Chunden, stayed with her to care for her and work with her as a porter. Ngorup entered school, where he studied English, Nepali, science, math, and civics.

One day, Jim heard about a relative of Ngorup's father who was looking for Ngorup in Kathmandu. When he met the man, he learned that the family was now planning to send Tubten Chundu, Ngorup's brother, to a Tibetan school in Kathmandu.

The man told Jim more about Ngorup's father. Ngorup's father had been one of a group of three Tibetan doctors, well known and respected before the Chinese attacked and took over Tibet in 1950. When the Chinese invaded, they rounded up all the doctors and intellectuals and threw them in jail, including the three doctors, who spent eighteen years in prison. During their imprisonment, the doctors kept to their religious faith, which had been threatened by the Chinese. Ngorup's father got out of jail sooner than the others. He then went to Thami in Nepal, where he met Lhakpa Dhiki. When the other two doctors were finally released, they left Tibet immediately and made their way to the Dalai Lama (Dahl-ee Lah-mah), the leader of the Buddhist faith, who was in exile in India. There, they spent several years recovering from their prison term. Then the Dalai Lama said to them, "Go to Kathmandu and start a college of Tibetan medicine that will serve the Kathmandu community."

So the two doctors traveled to Kathmandu, where they learned about Ngorup's brother, Tubten Chundu Sherpa. They called for him to come to Kathmandu, and one year his sister and mother brought him down from Thami. Tubten Chundu (nicknamed Tashi) was to enter the training school for doctors, but he was just five years old; so the family went to Jim's house for advice.

"The plan is for Tashi to become a Tibetan doctor like his father," explained Lhakpa Dhiki. "What do you think?"

Jim considered the situation. Finally he answered, "Yes, he should go and become a Tibetan doctor. He can always leave the medical school if he doesn't like it. But if he starts regular school, he will never leave there to become a Tibetan doctor." So Tashi entered the school, wearing tiny Buddhist robes.

Ngorup now thinks of Jim as a friend and stepfather, but he never loses track of his mother. He lives with Jim when he is not in school. If Jim returns to the United States to live, Ngorup will probably go with him, with his mother's blessing. He knows that he is a Sherpa and Jim is not. He keeps up his Buddhist faith and visits his brother, Tashi, at the Tibetan school in Kathmandu. The boys' oldest sister, Dolma, became a nun. Sometimes Ngorup asks Jim, "Why am I in Kathmandu? Why am I living with you?" And Jim explains, "So that you can send money to your mother when you are old enough." Ngorup likes the idea that he will be a wage earner and will be able to send money to his mother when he is older; he is now twelve.

Ngorup will probably never live in the Khumbu again, although he visits for months at a time. He worries about things that his friends in the Khumbu don't think about—passing his courses, moving on to the next grade, someday getting a job. But he knows he is important to his family. He has a new set of friends now as well as his own bicycle. Jim is teaching him how to trek and climb mountains. And he says that if he wants a yak, he'll "go to the Yak & Yeti Hotel." Over the years, Ngorup has crossed the line between two very different cultures. His life—and Jim's—have changed forever.

MOUNTAIN METHODS

A New Language

People all over the world speak different languages. Sometimes people within the same country speak different languages. In the United States, for example, various people in a single city may speak English, Spanish, or Chinese. In different areas of Nepal, people speak various languages as well, even though the official language of the country is Nepali. In the Khumbu, people may speak Nepali, Sherpa, Tibetan, and even a little English.

When you travel far from home, you do not need to be fluent in other languages in order to get along, but it helps to know a few words and phrases. Most times, the people in a place you visit will appreciate your effort to learn their language, and help you with it as best they can.

Written Nepali is based on Sanskrit, which is the written language of the Hindu people. Although you will not recognize the alphabet—the characters may look a little like Japanese or Chinese—many maps, restaurant menus, and some signs translate those characters into letters that you can read. The following are some useful Nepali phrases.

1. *Namaste* (nah-mah-stay). This is a friendly greeting that means "hello," "good-bye," and "how are you." Translated literally, it means "I salute the holiness within you."

2. *Taapai-ko naam ke ho* (tah-pie-ko nahm kay ho)? This asks, "What is your name?"

3. *Mero naam Linda ho* (mee-ro nahm Linda ho). This answers, "My name is Linda."

4. *Yo ke ho* (yo kay ho)? This asks, "What is this?"

5. *Chi cha* (chee chah)? This asks, "Is there tea?"

6. *Kattiko parchha* (kah-tee-ko par-chah)? This asks, "How much does it cost?"

7
A High-Altitude
Rescue Post

JIM FELL SILENT as we crunched along the frozen path toward Pheriche, surrounded by huge, deep-green rhododendrons, past a peaceful farm enclosed by a stone wall, and out into intense sunlight. We followed cairns (piles of rocks that marked the route) for a while, walking slowly. Time stretched ahead into the distance. I had no idea how fast we were traveling or how far we had come. We crossed a brown meadow littered with boulders, where the trail forked. To the right, the pale dirt path led off to Dingboche; to the left, the route led over the hill to Pheriche and perhaps help from the Himalayan Rescue Association.

We climbed the hill. At the top Jim stopped us. He pointed to a sliver of snow on the horizon.

"That's Island Peak," he announced. A thrill buzzed through my blood. There it was. After training for months and flying halfway around the world, we stood before the mountain. No way would I turn back now.

The trail sloped down toward the gushing river. We bounced across the rickety, suspended bridge to the other side, then marched up the hill to the village of Pheriche, at about fourteen thousand feet above sea level. A few stone buildings were scattered on either side of the dirt lane, and people ambled from one building to another. At the edge of town, we pushed open a gate and entered a dirt courtyard. A tiny, dumpy-looking building sat several feet back. The sign on the door read:

> Himalayan Rescue Association
> Tokyo Medical College
> Everest High Altitude Medical Institute

This was the Himalayan Rescue Association, the high-altitude rescue post that was built in 1973 by the Medical College of

Tokyo, Japan. The rescue post is now staffed mostly by American doctors who volunteer for three-month stints that correspond with the trekking and climbing season: February to April and September to December. The rescue post is usually closed during summer and winter.

At 3:30 in the afternoon we peered through the dusty glass window in the center of the door, then leaned on the door to open it, and stepped inside to find ourselves in the midst of a small crowd. A tall, thin man with dark hair and a beard, in a dirty blue parka, was giving a lecture. A group of trekkers and climbers, clad in filthy parkas, yak-wool caps, down pants, and scarves, sat around the room listening intently.

"The important thing to remember about altitude is that you must acclimatize," the speaker was saying. "Give your body time to adjust." We pressed around the outside of the group to the back of the room, where Jim whispered to another man who then motioned us to follow him into another room.

The man closed the door to the second room, dimming sound from the lecture. "I'm Ben Levine," he introduced himself. "I'm one of the doctors here." He was young, with red hair and a scraggly red beard. Wrapped in a rough wool scarf and an old navy-blue parka, he shuffled across the room in down booties. "Why don't you sit down?"

We sat in a line on the wooden bed at the side of the room. Ben asked me questions. He pushed the arms of my sweater up and looked at my skin, which was covered with hives. I pulled up my pants leg and showed him the same thing on my grimy shins. He aimed a penlight into my eyes and listened to my heart and breathing. He tapped the reflexes on my knees and ankles. Then he left and came back with some pills for me to take.

"I think you have an allergy to the cold," he explained. I was stunned. How could anyone possibly be allergic to the cold? I'd skied all my life, hiked and camped in the winter, and climbed ice. I'd never had this problem before. I'd also never heard of it. "Some people react like this when they exercise in the cold," he went on. "Something in the body triggers an allergic reaction." This sounded even more ridiculous. It felt unreal. I had trained for months and flown halfway around the world to have some doctor tell me that I was allergic to exercise in the cold. I just couldn't believe it. Then he dropped the bomb.

"This can be very dangerous. In fact, it could kill you. In addition to the allergy, you are starving. Your body has begun to feed on itself. You're a long way from a real hospital. I think you should consider turning around and going home." This was too much to take. I sat and stared at him. My stare turned to a glare.

"No," I said quietly.

Ben turned to Boyd. "If she were my wife, I'd take her home." Boyd said nothing, but squeezed my hand.

Ben saw how upset I was and tried to comfort me. "I know this is a big shock to you. But I want you to think about this carefully. Remember, you can always come back to the Himalaya. But if you die, you can't." I thought of a Sherpa saying I'd heard somewhere: "Go carefully. If you die, there is no second chance to climb."

I stiffened, resisting everything Ben said. I just wanted to be left alone. From what seemed like a long distance, I heard Jim saying, "I have to think about your safety. I can't let you go on if this is so serious."

"I'd like to be alone for a while," I mumbled. Ben nodded, and he and Jim left. For a while, I just sat still on the bed. Then I leaned back against the wall, and Boyd reached up to turn on the one lamp in the room. By now, the trekkers and climbers had cleared out of the building and there was silence. Jealousy coursed through me. All of these people were perfectly healthy, except for mild symptoms of mountain sickness. That I could handle. But how could something like this happen to me? I felt sorry for myself.

The medicine began to take effect, and the hives gradually disappeared. The itching died down. Boyd and I talked about the situation.

"One of us has to get to the top of the mountain. Maybe I should stay here while you climb with the rest of the guys, then meet you on the way down," I suggested halfheartedly. But I knew that Ben really wanted me to go home. I just couldn't accept it. Besides, if I stayed, there might not be anyone to help me if I had another attack—Ben and Bill, the other doctor, along with Bill's wife Judy, were going down to Tengboche for the Mani Rimdu festival.

The door opened and a young woman with blonde braids, glasses, and a light blue jacket entered.

"I'm Judy, Bill's wife," she said warmly. "I thought you might like a cup of tea." She handed me a plastic mug. "This is a big disappointment to you, isn't it?" I nodded. "We'd like you and

Boyd—and Jim, if he wants—to stay here with us tonight. You can sleep here in this room."

"Thank you," I said.

"Come and have dinner with us, in our quarters," she offered. "We don't have much—we don't even have electricity in there—but you have to eat and it might taste good." With the medicine taking effect, I realized that I was a little hungry, for the first time in days. Jim stuck his head inside the door.

"I'm going over the hill to Dingboche to see how the other guys are doing. Then I'll be back here to spend the night." He slipped out into the darkness, his light feet churning up the hill behind the rescue post.

Boyd and I followed Judy through a dark passageway and ducked into a cramped, square room lit by a candle stuck in a tin can. There was a window at one end and an old sink with a few cupboards nailed above it; but the building, like all other buildings in the Khumbu, had no running water. All water had to be hauled up from the river. Behind the flickering candle on the table sat Ben and Bill, who was splitting open tin cans with a can opener.

"Have a seat," said Bill as his hand rocked back and forth around the lid of a can. Boyd and I squeezed over to the far side, both of us sitting on one stool. Judy passed out plastic bowls. A Sherpa, who was standing at the sink with a large pot, came over to the table.

"This is Namka," said Ben.

Namka nodded toward us. "*Namaste,*" he said, sloshing a yellow liquid with noodles into my bowl.

"*Namaste,*" I answered. He reached across me and poured the same concoction into Boyd's dish, then Judy, Bill, and Ben's. Namka and another Sherpa, Ang Rita, assisted Bill and Ben at the rescue association. Namka had gone on many high-altitude expeditions. He had walked through the deadly Khumbu Icefall at the base of Everest fifty-two times. When an ultralight aircraft crashed into the river several years ago, it looked as though rescuers would have to walk at least a mile before they could cross the river to reach the victims. But Namka raced to the river with an aluminum expedition ladder and anchored it across the gorge so that the rescuers could reach the victims in time to save their lives.

I lifted a cold spoon and dipped it into the lukewarm soup. I cut a few noodles with the edge of the spoon and took a bite. It tasted salty and good. I took a few more bites of noodles awash in soup.

My stomach remained quiet. Ben and Bill talked about their duties at the rescue post. The two loved to climb and had come to Nepal to climb in the Himalaya and to give medical care to both tourists and Sherpas in the Khumbu. Bill, who was an emergency-room doctor back home, had just returned from climbing a local peak. Ben was especially interested in the effects of altitude on the body. He was also interested in this business about allergy to the cold. Judy was a physical therapist in the United States and assisted Ben and Bill at the rescue post.

They explained that all medicines and supplies are donated to the Himalayan Rescue Association, so they could only treat people with whatever medicine happened to be on hand. It was lucky that they had the right medicine for me; otherwise, they would not have been able to help. The Himalayan Rescue Association asks trekkers and climbers for a donation for treatment and medicine; it treats Sherpas for free.

Ben passed around a tin of tuna. I stuck my fork into it and took a bite of the tangy, oily fish. It was good. That was all I could eat, but it was a start.

I lay awake that night, unable to sleep. Ben came in to give me another pill, and gradually I was feeling better. I knew that the situation was serious, but deep down I felt that if we could get it under control, I would be fine. I simply didn't believe that I was allergic to cold. Jim had returned and was sleeping on the bench in the main room of the building, buried deep in his sleeping bag. Earlier, when he had come back, he had slipped into the room and given me a note that read: "Hope you're feeling better soon." It was signed by Jimmy, Allen, and George. The note made me feel stronger. We were becoming a team.

In the morning, Boyd and I made our way through the cold passageway to the kitchen again. Jim set out over the hill to re-trieve the others and bring them back to Pheriche. I wolfed down a large bowl of sticky porridge with raisins. I drank plenty of tea. My appetite was back.

"Ben wants you to stay here this morning," Bill informed me.

"Where is he?" I asked.

"Sick," answered Bill. Ben had developed a stomach bug and spent the night running between bed and the outhouse.

I found a book and settled into the main room to wait for my medicine. The room was cramped and square. A rusted wood stove in the center provided the only heat in the building. To my left was a desk with a window above it. A chart on the wall described the symptoms of mountain sickness. Above the door hung the broken wood propeller of the ultralight that Namka had rescued. Along the wall beside the desk was the clinic's library of paperbacks left by climbers, including a lot of mountaineering books. The most ragged of these was *Mountain Sickness* by Peter Hackett. Various stickers, badges, newspaper clippings, and even a map of the New York subway system lined the other walls. Taped to the back wall were scraps of paper saying "no smoking" in twenty different languages. One was even written by Jimmy Carter. Medical supplies occupied the shelves in the back corner, and half a dozen stethoscopes hung from a nylon cord strung from one end of the room to another.

At about 8:00, the bright yak bell hanging above the door sounded, announcing the first patient. Then trekkers seemed to arrive all at once, swarming into the room with complaints of headaches, light-headedness, nausea, earaches, and diarrhea. All of them asked about mountain sickness. Bill examined each of them, sending some on their way with medicine, and all of them on their way with encouraging words. A couple whom we had met on the plane to Lukla walked in and asked how I was feeling. News travels fast along the trail.

The Himalayan Rescue Association is devoted to educating trekkers and climbers about the effects of altitude on the body. Every day at 3:00, one of the doctors gives a lecture about acclimatizing (adjusting to altitude) and acute mountain sickness, which is a risk to anyone who travels high in the mountains. Many people in past years have become ill and died from acute mountain sickness. The doctors know that the best treatment is prevention so they educate as many people who come through the area as they can.

By now, Boyd was showing signs of mild mountain sickness, which meant that his body was not adjusting quickly enough to the altitude. He felt weak, weary, and short of breath. But he did not have the most common symptom—the headache. Allen, on the other hand, had had a headache and shortness of breath for several days. Both were experiencing the same illness because their bodies had not acclimatized.

The door opened once again and in clomped George, Allen, and Jimmy. Jimmy threw his arms around me and hugged me hard.

"We were worried about you. We decided we weren't going anywhere without you. We're going to camp here until you're ready to climb."

"Thanks," I answered, smiling.

Allen patted me on the back, grinning through his blonde beard. "You're OK, kid. You're going to make it."

Then Allen turned to Bill and described his symptoms of mountain sickness. Bill gave him a medicine called Diamox to reduce the extra fluid the body holds at high altitude. It can help get rid of a headache and edema, or swelling.

Ben shuffled in, wearing red down pants and a scarf flung around his mouth and nose.

"Hi," he said, his voice muffled by the scarf. "How are you feeling?"

"Pretty good," I answered. "Actually, a lot better. I think I'm going to be fine. How are you?"

"Terrible. And we'll see about you." He handed me a pill. Jim came into the room. "I'd like to try something," Ben continued. "Jim, can you get me a basin of cold water? I want to try a cold challenge." A grin eased across Jim's mouth and he went outside. A few minutes later he returned carrying a huge basin of water from the river, with sheets of ice floating on top. I looked at Ben.

"Come in here," he said, and we moved to the other room. I rolled up my sleeve and plunged my right arm into the water, up to my elbow. Boyd took photos and Ben timed me for two minutes. He wanted to see if my arm would break out in hives. When the two minutes were up, I pulled out my arm in triumph. There was no reaction. Just a cold arm. Now Ben would have to let me go.

"OK," Ben agreed. "Things are looking good. This afternoon, I want you to take a test hike, in the snow. Don't stray too far from here. See what happens."

So Boyd, Jim, and I set out, marching up into clouds as curtains of snow billowed around us. I felt fine. Along the edge of the hill, we heard a snort: ahead stood a huge Tibetan yak.

"That's a Cadillac yak!" exclaimed Boyd. The yak shuddered and turned to stare at us. He flicked his shaggy tail and snow flew from the fur. We steered around him and headed down the hill, back to the rescue association. Judy had started a fire in the wood stove. As we shed wet wool, it steamed in the warmth. I checked my arms and legs. No hives. I was home free.

That night, we gathered in the main room of the clinic with Ben, Bill, and Judy for dinner. Pasang and his crew set up the table in the center of the room, and cedar logs burned fragrantly in the stove. The single bare lightbulb snapped on. We passed around bowls of broth and cups of tea; then we served up fried noodles, curry, and gravy, finishing up with canned fruit cocktail. My appetite was back and I was determined to prove to Ben that I was healthy. I ate like a horse. Ben had probably saved my life, and so had Boyd; but I wasn't ready to admit that yet. It was too scary a thought.

We camped in the frosty yard across the lane from the Himalayan Rescue Association. I slept well for the first time in many nights. The next morning, Ben handed me a packet of medicine.

"This should be enough to get you through the trip. But be careful," he warned. "And, by the way, don't take aspirin or antacid tablets. Sometimes people suddenly develop allergic reactions to those, too."

I stuffed the envelope in my pocket. "Thank you," I replied, and embraced him in a quick hug. Then, like a bird let out of its cage, I was gone, flying across the valley, over bright red flowers, toward the Khumbu Glacier—and Island Peak.

MOUNTAIN METHODS

The Effects of Altitude

Altitude, or elevation, is the height of a place above sea level. As you climb higher and higher, the air contains less oxygen. At eighteen thousand feet elevation, for example, the air contains one-half the amount of oxygen it does at sea level. This has several effects on your body; the most important involve breathing, blood circulation, and water balance.

You can help minimize these effects by *acclimatizing,* or giving your body time to adjust to the change in altitude. Everyone is different; some people acclimatize more quickly than others. Physical fitness has *nothing* to do with acclimatizing. No matter how strong you are, you must always give your body a chance to adjust.

If your body does not acclimatize, you may develop *acute mountain sickness.* Mountain sickness may be mild or very serious, so always pay attention to its symptoms. Severe mountain sickness can kill you.

Symptoms

Symptoms of acute mountain sickness are headache, light-headedness, sleeplessness, loss of coordination, swelling in the eyes and face, cough, shortness of breath, loss of appetite, nausea and vomiting, weakness and weariness, a heavy feeling in the legs, and reduced urine output. A person may have just a few of these symptoms or many of them.

Treatment

The best treatment for acute mountain sickness is descent—going lower in altitude so that the body can recover. You can try aspirin for a headache and cough drops for a cough. Drink water until your urine becomes colorless. But if none of these things works, don't climb any higher; at least stay where you are. If the symptoms persist, go down until your body acclimatizes. There are medications that help reduce the symptoms of acute mountain sickness, but they must be prescribed by a doctor.

Prevention

The best way to prevent mountain sickness is by acclimatizing. Make a gradual ascent once you are above nine thousand feet. If you climb a thousand feet in one day, stay at the same altitude the following day; then move on if your body has adjusted. Drink lots of fluids and eat foods high in carbohydrates. (See "Mountain Methods: What to Eat on Your Mountaineering Trip" following chapter 4.)

8
Onto the
Khumbu Glacier

WE TRAMPED ACROSS the valley floor, beneath the knife-edge summit of Lobuche (Lo-beh-chay) Peak. Then the route curved to the east, onto a wide steep hill like a barren ski slope. We dug our boots into the dry dirt, tacking back and forth toward the top. Then the hill rounded out. Ahead lay the Khumbu Glacier, leading to the base of Mt. Everest.

I had expected the glacier to be a huge mass of cold blue-green ice; but instead it was a wild tumble of rocky debris with gray dust rising from every footstep. Hidden under this layer of rock lies the ice, moving slowly down the valley; the Khumbu Glacier is still active. With a shout, we stepped onto the loose rock, stumbling among boulders, wading through scree. George sped ahead, his long legs striding smoothly over the stones.

Near midday, we stopped at a building surrounded by a stone wall. There George sat in the yard, reading. Zangbu and Kami, two of Pasang's kitchen boys, emerged from the dark doorway and motioned us inside the yard. The yaks were already loose, ambling around, nuzzling the ground for something to eat. I opened the gate and a huge yak swung its heavy head around to stare at me, its horns gleaming in the sun. I stepped around it carefully.

The greasy orange plastic sheet that served as our tablecloth was spread on the ground, held down at the corners by four stones. Jimmy pulled off his wool cap and lay down at one end of the cloth, his brown hair crushed and matted. He soon fell fast asleep. Boyd, Allen, and I leaned against the wall. Jim was slightly behind us; he had stayed in Pheriche to take care of some business.

Pasang cried, "Lunch!" from inside the house. Jimmy woke from his nap and George put away his book. We plunged our hands into the basin of violet disinfectant that the kitchen crew laid out for us before each meal. Then Pasang appeared with a plate of freshly baked *chappattis,* a dish of stewed tomatoes, fried egg-plant, and tea. Dawa offered cups of hot orange squash.

After lunch, we spread our map of the Khumbu on the ground and studied it.

"Here's Lobuche, where we're headed tonight," said Allen, tracing his gloved finger along the purple line of the map. "We'll be following the Khumbu Glacier all day."

"Here's Kala Pattar," pointed out Jimmy. "I guess we climb that tomorrow." Kala Pattar is the "black rock" that lies below Pumori (Poo-mor-ee), at 18,500 feet. It was a nontechnical climb that we planned to do as a warmup before attempting Island Peak.

George went back to reading his book. He read a lot during the trip. Since he was such a fast hiker, he often reached the group's destination before we did, so he had plenty of time to settle in and read. Although he ran a large hotel in Yellowstone Park, he longed to become an English teacher. He was also by far the strongest and most experienced climber in our group; he had climbed many peaks in the Colorado Rockies and in the Grand Tetons of Wyoming.

As Dendi and Kancha rounded up the yaks, Jettha rose with his stick and deftly got them in line. The animals plodded out of the yard and onto the trail. As we gathered our packs, a distant buzzing grew louder and louder. We looked up at the sky: a plane was coming toward us. This was unusual; planes don't fly over the Himalaya because the mountains are too high and the air is too thin.

Anu stared for a few minutes, then declared, "Tourists."

"You mean tourists can hire a plane for sightseeing?" asked Boyd.

"Yes," answered Anu. "They are very rich."

Even from a distance, the noise of the plane penetrated the deep silence of the Himalaya, shaking us to the core. We had not heard a motor of any kind since leaving Lukla. And once we had passed the larger villages, we simply heard the clanging of yak bells and shouts of yak drivers—and occasionally the ominous rumble of an avalanche or rock fall. Mostly, we heard nothing at all.

Scattered along the trail, we walked up the Khumbu Glacier toward Lobuche. The voice of a young Sherpani singing drifted down from somewhere in the hills. Yaks paced the side of the wide, brown slope. Ahead lay Pumori—"daughter peak"—its dazzling white summit stark against the sky. Suddenly, a yak got loose from a young driver and Anu and Dendi scrambled to help round it up.

Anu, our sirdar, *on the left; Dendi, one of our climbing Sherpas, on the right.*

"Psooweet! Psooweet! Aywhayah ayahuh!" they cried. The yak driver tossed a rock, clipping the yak in the ankle and spinning it around toward the right direction. Anu and Dendi laughed.

We marched along the gully cut by the huge glacier. The air was growing thin and cold as we climbed higher and higher. The path crossed a motionless stream, its water nearly congealed into ice. Dendi leapt off the trail and waded into snow by the stream bank. He stomped around, then bent over, making sweeping motions with his arms. When he stood back, he revealed a word written in Sanskrit in the snow: *Sagarmatha.* During the late 1800's, explorers, surveyors (men who explored and then made maps of the areas they explored), and mountaineers worked their way into the Himalaya. They discovered that the tallest mountain in the world lay in Nepal, on the border near Tibet. The surveyors first gave this mountain a number, Peak XV (Peak 15). Then they named the mountain after a British official who made surveys of the Himalaya: George Everest. But Mt. Everest already had a name. The Tibetans called it Chomolungma (Goddess Mother of the World). Later, the Nepalese gave it their own name: Sagarmatha (Goddess Mother of the Snows).

Along the trail, we passed seventeen monuments to Sherpas who had died in the Khumbu Icefall. The icefall is a break in the slope of the Khumbu Glacier, which flows down from Mt. Everest. As the ice creeps over this break, it cracks into enormous blocks that move as the glacier moves, sometimes toppling over and crashing down the mountain. People who climb Everest from this side must walk from base camp through the icefall to get onto the mountain; many consider this to be the most dangerous part of the climb. A number of those who have perished on Everest have died in the Khumbu Icefall. Anu explained, "So many people died, we asked the lama at Tengboche for a blessing. We had a ceremony at base camp. We offered prayer flags and scattered rice. Now not so many Sherpas die in the icefall." But new monuments would be added this fall; more Sherpas had already died.

Way up the trail there was a black dot in the middle of the snow. As we grew closer, the dot became George, perched on a rock near the icy stream, reading. His socks and T-shirt were spread in the sun, drying. He had hiked so fast that he had decided to stop and do his laundry while he waited for the rest of us. He looked up from his book and waved.

"Go ahead," he shouted. "I'll catch up."

As light drained from the sky and fog rolled in, we heard the swift steps of someone running barefoot down the trail. A Sherpa flew by us, bouncing a larger man on his back. The climber had developed severe mountain sickness and the quickest way to get him down to a lower altitude was to run with him piggyback.

We pulled into Lobuche at dusk. Lobuche is a popular camping spot; people sleep there before and after they climb Kala Pattar or Lobuche Peak itself. Tents and campfires were strewn about in the dusk. Yaks wandered through the shallow stream, slurping glacial water. Tea bags, cellophane wrappers, cardboard boxes, toilet paper, tin cans, coffee grinds, and orange peels littered the ground and the stream. Garbage was heaped everywhere; muddy, frozen ashes from fires were clumped together in the dirt. Even the outhouse was full and brimming; I gagged when I walked in. Although we pitched our own toilet tent downstream, our efforts were useless; there were plenty of latrines upstream as well, and waste would just wash down through all the camps. Huge groups had moved through and left trash everywhere. One of the problems in the Himalaya is that if groups don't remove their own trash, there is nowhere to put it. It just lies on the ground and in the streams, frozen.

After unrolling my sleeping bag, I stuck my head inside Allen and Jimmy's tent. They greeted me with groans. Allen had a sick stomach and Jimmy had a bad cold. But they crawled out and followed me to the kitchen tent for tea.

Pasang appeared with *makai* (popcorn), charred and crunchy. We passed the pot around, craving the salt on the popcorn.

Purba ducked into the tent with a pot of tea.

"*Taapai-ko naam ke ho?*" I asked, trying my Nepali.

Startled, he replied, "*Mero naam Purba Sherpa.*" I was equally surprised that he understood me.

"*Mero naam Linda ho,*" I said. That was all the Nepali I knew (except for "How much does that cost?" and "What is that?"), so I didn't know what to say next. But he smiled and nodded, handing me the heavy pot of tea.

While we ate popcorn and waited for Jim, a yak wandered over to the door of the tent and dipped its muzzle into the bowl of disinfectant lying there. At the sound of gentle lapping, Jimmy flung open the tent.

"Ho!" he shouted, and the yak lifted its head, violet water dripping from its mouth. It couldn't have tasted very good.

Jim arrived. While walking up the trail, he had learned from a passing friend that Ngorup's older sister, Dolma, had died at age seventeen, from unknown causes. The doctor at the Khunde hospital did not find out in time that she was sick; and after she died, he was not allowed to examine her body. Sherpas tend to cover up death, preferring not to talk about it. But they also believe in reincarnation, which means they will live again, so they do not mourn their dead in the same way that we do.

After dinner, we returned to our tents. Morning tea was scheduled for 4:00, so we could get an early start for the summit of Kala Pattar. I stuffed all my outer clothes and my water bottle into the foot of my sleeping bag to keep them warm. The temperature had dropped steadily as we had climbed, and there would be no more warm nights for several weeks. It was mid-November, and the temperature was only eighteen degrees at 8:00 that night. I put on my wool cap to keep as much of my body heat in as possible, and yanked the drawstring tight on my sleeping bag. Outside, the Sherpas sang folksongs, beating a steady rhythm on drums. Smoke drifted through camp, wafting into the tent. I thought I would be nervous about climbing Kala Pattar—18,500 feet was higher than I'd ever been—but I wasn't. I felt strong and healthy—and grateful to be here, still climbing. The altitude had not begun to bother me yet, and already we were sleeping at sixteen thousand feet above sea level. But Boyd was fighting the altitude. "My legs feel like lead weights when I walk," he said. He was acclimatizing a day or two behind everyone else, so just as he felt fit, we moved on and the struggle began again. But he never let his spirits lag behind.

Thoughts of tomorrow's climb faded. We lay in the dark, listening to the drone of chants and drums, gliding off to sleep.

MOUNTAIN METHODS

Life Outdoors: Camping

The key to good camping is learning to live outdoors. When you camp, the outdoors is your neighborhood. Your tent is your house and your sleeping bag is your bed. Your camping stove is your kitchen. It is important to treat the outdoors carefully. When you leave a campsite, whether it's in a campground or in the backcountry, no one should be able to tell that you were there.

Setting Up Camp

Choose and set up your campsite before dark, so that you can see. Make sure that you are in an area where camping is allowed. Try to find a level campsite in an area where rainwater won't collect. If you're in an open area such as a field, try to find the most protected spot. Locate your site at least a hundred feet away from a stream or pond. Don't cut live branches. Spread a plastic sheet across your tent floor to keep it dry.

Cooking Meals

It is much safer and better for the environment to use a camping stove instead of building a fire. (In fact, some areas don't allow fires at all.) Use your stove in an area that isn't too windy, but *never* use it in your tent, no matter how bad the weather is. Try to wash dishes with hot water, but keep soap away from a stream or pond. If you must build a fire, keep it small. Use only dead wood, and make sure the ashes are cool before leaving the campsite.

Settling In for the Night

Leave your backpack outside or under the fly of the tent, with your food in it and the zippers undone; it's better to have chipmunks only eat your food than rip through your pack *before* they eat your food. If you're in an area with bears, hang your food in trees in stuff-sacks. Take your boots off before you slide all the way into the tent to keep dirt and dampness outside. Remove your socks and spread them out or hang them on a cord to dry. You can stash your next day's clothes at the bottom of your sleeping bag to keep them warm and dry. Slip your flashlight and toilet paper into the side pocket of your tent or within reach.

Pack It In, Pack It Out

Burn any toilet paper you use. Carry out all your trash in plastic bags that can be resealed so that they don't leak.

9
Kala Pattar:
The Black Rock

LONG BEFORE DAWN, the dull jets of Pasang's cookstove hissed through my dreams. All night, Pasang had been baking bread and cake for us to carry to Kala Pattar. Now he could go to bed. Pasang, the kitchen boys, and Anu were staying in camp today. I sat up, reached for my headlamp, and unzipped the tent flap to check the thermometer that hung just outside: fifteen degrees. Twenty feet away, the shadows of Pasang and his crew fluttered in the lantern light against the walls of the cook tent. The heavy flap of the tent flopped open and Dendi appeared, carrying a steaming pot of tea over the hard, frosty earth.

"*Namaste,*" he whispered hoarsely. He bent and poured tea into two plastic cups.

"Thank you, Dendi," I said, and retreated into the tent, handing a cup to Boyd.

After a quick breakfast of muesli (oat flakes) splashed with hot, watery *dudh,* we moved stiffly out into the cold morning. As I bent to cinch my parka to the outside of my pack, blood rushed to my head and I nearly tipped over. I squatted on the ground for a moment, letting my head clear. I looked around at the rest of the group. This was the first day we'd be climbing in heavy clothes: sweaters, anoraks, and wool caps, pants, and gloves.

Still chilled to the bone, we trudged up the cold valley in pale light. A fourteen-hour nontechnical climb lay ahead of us, including the hike back to Lobuche. We would gain 2,500 feet in elevation in the climb to the 18,500-foot–high summit. There, the air would contain less than half the oxygen it contains at sea level. This was a personal test for each of us: it was the highest climb any of us had ever made, and it would also serve as our first warm-up climb for Island Peak.

The deep silence of the Himalaya engulfed me like a glass jar.

Sometimes, I thought, *the silence is so intense that it has its own sound.* In the Himalaya, I didn't strain to distinguish among sounds; I strained to distinguish among different types of silence.

As the chill left my muscles, I lengthened my stride. Pale yellow light crept across the massive Nuptse wall looming to the right. The trail angled upward, edging along the side of a rock pile. As I clambered among boulders, flames of heat shot through my calves and upper legs. I lifted my hands, placing them on my waist to give my lungs more room to breathe. I walked in the climbing rhythm: breathe, breathe, step. I wound my scarf around my mouth to moisten the air and keep the dust and searing cold from my throat. I coughed and broke my pace. Then I stopped and turned, looking back down the glacier valley. Three tiny figures inched toward me: Jim, Dendi, and Boyd. Jimmy, Allen, George, Nima, and Kancha were now well ahead of us.

Boyd and Dendi reached me and we shared a drink of water and a fruit bar. Then Dendi took the lead, darting back and forth as the route snaked among the boulders and across scree. He swiftly disappeared. I picked my way through the rock, placing each step deliberately without losing my pace. One slip now could mean a plummet down the rock pile into the valley. If I were lucky, this might result only in a broken ankle; but it would dash any hopes for climbing Island Peak.

Jim was still far behind us, but hiking swiftly. I looked ahead at the rocks strewn willy-nilly, huge pillars of stone, boulders teetering on the edge of the slope. It was as if a giant had dropped a handful of stones from the sky. The route was a maze, the cairns blending into their surroundings. Soon I was alone, although I knew that Boyd and Dendi were somewhere near as I caught glimpses of color as their jackets appeared and disappeared behind boulders. What a great place this would be to play hide-and-seek.

Then the route became a slim path leading down a slope to a flat brown meadow. At the bottom lay a lonely tea house with a curl of smoke seeping out of its doorway. (Houses in Nepal don't have chimneys.) A stone wall enclosed a slab of barren ground outside the house. George, Jimmy, Allen, and Kancha were stretched in the sun along the wall, waiting for me. I hailed them from the top of the hill and strode down to meet them.

"Is this Gorak Shep?" I asked.

"Yep," answered Jimmy, stretching and yawning.

Gorak Shep means "dead crow." It is one of the highest settlements in the world, at seventeen thousand feet above sea level, although people do not live there in the winter. (Humans cannot live year-round above seventeen thousand feet because their bodies weaken after being at high altitude for too long.) We were to meet there for lunch. I shrugged off my pack and dropped it on the ground. I undid the laces of my boots to give my feet some breathing room. (The higher I climbed, the more my feet swelled, due to the altitude.) Then I leaned against the wall to soak up the sun. Nima came out of the tea house carrying several cups of tea, his fingers looped through the handles. Behind us an expanse of white sand, like a beach, led to an enormous barren hill that sloped up to Kala Pattar. Breeze swirled the sand into dust devils, carrying it off over the glacier. From here we could only see the false summit (a closer, lower summit blocking the true summit) of Kala Pattar—a jagged, triangular peak like a giant cairn. The true summit, a narrow black spit of rock, lay hidden.

Jim, Boyd, and Dendi tromped down the trail as Nima unwrapped the cake and bread that Pasang had sent along with Dendi. The bread was thick and tasty. The cake, dark brown and heavy, tasted of molasses and ginger. We craved sweets in the cold; our bodies burned the calories quickly in an effort to keep warm. We'd begun to dream of hot apple pie and rich chocolate cake, and we swore we'd gorge ourselves, traveling from restaurant to restaurant, when we returned to Kathmandu. But for now, Pasang's cake was a treat.

We downed the cake, bread, dried fruit, and granola bars along with several cups of tea. Then we packed up for the final climb. I adjusted my backpack on my shoulders, cinching the straps so that it was evenly balanced on my back. We chugged up the hill, following rivulets of brown trail as it wound back and forth toward the sky. Clumps of withered grass clung to the dry soil. By now, we could not even see the false summit of Kala Pattar; it was blocked by the hill. But to the east, across the Khumbu Glacier, stood Everest, Lhotse, and Nuptse, their summits cold and harsh in the bright sun. The south col (a gap in the mountain ridge) of Everest gleamed like a knife and the "yellow band," faint stripes of iron-stained limestone near the summit, glowed softly. There were no expeditions on Everest now, for the government of Nepal closes the mountain to climbers for the month of November. Ironically, this year's fall expeditions had been filled with frustration and disaster because of bad weather. But now, when climbing was not allowed, the weather had been brilliant for weeks. Below the great peaks lay the empty expanse of glacier called Everest Base Camp. No one lives at the base camp; it is just the place where expeditions establish their base of operations. Wind blew across the haunting, empty camp, calling up images of all the successful and unsuccessful, famous and not-so-famous mountaineers who had come to try their luck and skill on Everest. Each expedition requires months of planning, tons of food and gear, sometimes months of waiting at base camp and working on the mountain—with no promise of success and occasionally even tragedy. The size of the project is staggering. As I gazed at the mountain and the windswept camp, I was filled with new respect for those who had tried.

I continued up the hill, striving for my own summit. For some reason, the higher I climbed, the better I felt. If I moved slowly and deliberately, the fuzziness in my head cleared and I felt strong. My ankles ached from bending so far over to keep upright on the steep slope. I leaned into the hill, head down, forgetting the view for a

Everest, center, looks smaller than Nuptse because it is farther away. Below Everest the Khumbu Icefall tumbles onto the glacier, where base camp lies.

while. I hooked my hands into my side pockets, giving my lungs every ounce of oxygen they could suck in. Above me, George, Allen, and Jimmy mounted the rock cone leading to the summit of Kala Pattar. Kancha stood at the base of the cone, waiting for me in the blue pile jacket that Jerry had given him in thanks for guiding him and Linda back to Lukla. My thoughts wandered back to Jerry and Linda. I wondered whether they had made it home by now; their departure from the group seemed like a year ago.

I met Kancha and he motioned me to step onto the rock cone. The huge pile of stone, polished black by millions of years of wind and snow, soared nearly a thousand feet high. My boots wobbled on loose, flat slabs and I searched for handholds, hoisting myself up ledge after ledge. Kancha darted up easily, following me. All the Sherpas live above ten thousand feet and grow up climbing this kind of terrain. So this was like climbing in their backyard. Wind sailed up the cone, knocking me off balance, challenging every step I made. I stopped often, peering ahead, straining to find the cairns. The route was like an uncrackable code.

Breathing hard, I turned to Kancha. "Would you lead?" I pleaded. He took over. I followed, pushing against the wind, stepping across gaps, boosting myself up on the next ledge. I stopped for a rest and Kancha unzipped my pack, reaching in for my water bottle. I spun open the top and drank as blood pounded in my ears. The pounding grew louder, into a rumble. Far off, out of sight, an avalanche poured down the flanks of a mountain.

Ready for the final push, we climbed higher and higher, scrambling over boulders, walking out to the brink of the cone, hauling ourselves toward the sky. Above, Jimmy, George, and Allen reached the summit and descended again to safer ground; there was room only for one or two people on the needle-like peak. Then Boyd came up behind me and together we inched our way up to the top. Jim took our picture from below as we huddled together, grinning in the wind.

We gathered below on a large ledge and broke out packets of dried fruit and granola. We gulped ice-cold water as Jim pointed out some of the peaks in the distance.

"That small, square peak over there is in Tibet," he told us. "But I don't remember its name."

"Well, we've got Nuptse here, and Lhotse over there," said Allen.

"Then I name the unknown peak Whoopsie," declared Jimmy. He looked around. "Where's George?"

"Climbing Whoopsie," Boyd replied. "He was bored with Kala Pattar."

We pressed together for a group photograph as Boyd opened his tripod and set the timer on his camera. Then he leapt into the picture as the camera snapped, freezing our smiles.

Soon we took off down the cone, swiftly but steadily descending. The wind increased, battering our legs and jackets. George, like a mountain goat, was gone within minutes, with Jimmy close behind. Allen followed carefully; the altitude had made him lightheaded. The run-out down Kala Pattar was steep and vast, so we kept our minds alert to the task. One slip could mean a fall of several thousand feet.

My legs ached as we reached the Khumbu Glacier and dropped below the hills, behind the wind. Afternoon fog eased in, filling the valley with a soft gray chill. In the distance, another avalanche rumbled down another mountain, and exhaustion settled on our shoulders. But we had taken our first test in the Himalaya, and we had passed it.

MOUNTAIN METHODS

Tips for Hiking

Hiking may seem as natural as walking. But hiking involves carrying a backpack, climbing rough terrain, and walking for long periods of time. For example, carrying a pack feels a bit like riding a bicycle with someone else on back. Once you get used to the extra weight, you automatically adjust your balance. With a few tips, hiking *will* become as natural as walking.

1. Adjust your pack so that it sits high up, comfortably on your shoulders. It is easier to move freely when you carry your weight closer to your shoulders than to your waist. If you need to strap a piece of equipment (such as a tent) to your pack, strap it tightly to the top rather than the bottom. Don't let extra gear dangle on the outside of your pack; it will throw you off balance as you walk.

2. Plant your feet firmly, using the entire sole of each foot without stomping. Move evenly so that you can reverse any step if you lose your balance.

3. Watch for damp logs, wet leaves, and slick rocks. They can send you flying down the trail. Try to walk around them if possible.

4. When climbing a steep hill, rest your hands on your hips or tuck them under your pack straps. This allows your lungs to breathe more easily.

5. When walking downhill, control your pace so that you don't skid off the trail. A long, fast descent can really pound your knees and ankles.

6. Stop for water and snacks. It is better to stop often for ten minutes than to stop once in a while for half an

hour. A long rest can cause your muscles to stiffen and cramp.

7. If you choose to carry a walking stick, use it to help you maintain your balance and walking rhythm, but don't lean your full weight on it. If you are traversing (walking across) a hillside, carry the stick in your uphill hand.

10
Crossing the Glacier

PASANG HAD A RADIO. After breakfast the next morning, he set it on the ground and turned the dial till we could barely hear Radio Nepal news through the blur of static. Radio Nepal news comes on at 8:00 A.M. and mostly concerns the social comings and goings of the king and queen of Nepal. We sat in the sun and listened for a while, until the twangy music of India whined and droned through the air.

Jim came over to where we were lounging. "Come on, let's clean this place up," he encouraged. He produced an old, moldy basket into which we could toss trash. We scoured the entire camp area at Lobuche, combing abandoned campsites for trash that could be burned. We wanted to leave Lobuche a little cleaner than we had found it, if possible.

I waded into the stream, picking up soaked tea bags and cellophane wrappers from the near-freezing water. We raked through old campfires for boxes and empty cans, which we crushed and dropped in a pile. Then we threw all the burnable trash into a pit near the stream and lit a thick, black smoky fire. We surveyed our work. Lobuche still looked like the town dump. But we had tried.

Steam rose from the earth, curling upward as the sun warmed the ground. Feeling especially grubby after nearly two weeks on the trail, we decided to try giving ourselves shampoos. Pasang put a large kettle on the kitchen fire and soon we had hot water. Allen went first. He bent over as I poured a stream of water over his head, soaking his hair. Then Boyd balanced the kettle over my head as I bent way over with a towel thrown around my neck. The stream of warm water seeped into my scalp. I rubbed a small amount of shampoo through my hair, scrubbing as hard as I could, trying to cut through the dirt. Then I bent over again as Boyd poured a river of water through by hair to rinse it. I flipped my hair back in the sun and drew a comb through it; immediately, snow formed on the comb and in my hair! It was only 32 degrees, but we were getting so used to the cold that it felt like spring!

We broke camp late in the morning and started our trek toward the Khumbu Glacier. We would cross the glacier today and pitch camp on the other side, in a meadow called Ling-Ten. Tomorrow was our second shakedown climb: crossing the Kongma-La, the 18,200-foot–high pass leading into the Imja Valley.

We hiked across dark mounds of coal-black moraine (deposits of rock from the glacier) to reach the edge of the Khumbu Glacier. There, we stood looking down into a teeming tumble of boulders and gravel sparkling with mica dust. Here and there cairns were scattered; we thought they might mark the route across the glacier to the base of the Kongma-La, but we weren't sure. We spread our map on the ground, trying to line it up with landmarks and Ling-Ten. Boyd oriented his compass to the map and our vague direction.

"I'll lead for a while," Allen offered. We folded the map. He had a job ahead of him since the few cairns that existed blended in with the surroundings. And we weren't even sure they led to the right place.

We started down the narrow trail, slipping and sliding in the loose gravel as it dropped steeply to the floor of the glacier. I looked around. Heaps of rock rose a hundred feet in the air. The thread of trail followed the floor of the valley for a while before making an upward slant toward the next wave of rock. Then it vanished. The glacier gave us few clues to direction, but our compass told us to keep heading southeast, toward Ling-Ten.

Dust settled in my hair, my mouth, my nose, and behind my glacier glasses. I did not want to stop for a drink because I knew that as soon as I opened my bottle, dust would land in the water. We leapt from boulder to boulder along the crest of the third moraine and stopped to rest. At the head of the glacier lay Pumori, glistening in the sun. Behind us, flowing down the valley, the glacier led almost to Pheriche.

Dendi leaned against a rock, his hands in his jacket pockets. Anu moved slightly away, fingering his wooden prayer beads. The sound of his mutterings to Buddha drifted back to us. Soon he stopped and joined us again.

"Praying?" I asked.

He smiled and nodded, then waved his arm at Everest. In 1973, he had climbed to twenty-six thousand feet on the south col of

Everest as a high-altitude porter with an Italian expedition. The expedition was organized by a wealthy nobleman, and it was so large and lavish that base camp was established at Lukla. The nobleman insisted that climbers and other important members of the group be flown to the base of Everest by a helicopter. But the air was so thin at seventeen thousand feet that once the helicopter dropped off its passengers, it could not take off again. The Italians abandoned it on the ice.

In 1981, Anu served as base-camp *sirdar* for the attempt at Everest from the Lho-La on the northwest side. "When there are Sherpas, I am in charge," he declared. "Sometimes there are two groups of Sherpas—one climbing, one at base camp. On the Lho-La expedition, the team got to within a hundred yards of the summit. Then the leader said to turn around because it was too late to reach the top and come down safely, before dark. I think this is success in a climb. When no lives are lost, that is success."

Anu stood still at the top of the moraine, gazing at Everest, fingering his earth-colored beads as he spoke. His gold tooth flashed in the sun. "When we are climbing," he went on, "all the team must work together. If five fingers are together, you can catch. If one finger is not together, you drop."

A hollow rumble sounded two hundred feet below us and Anu whistled. Thinking it was another avalanche, we looked around wildly for its source. Anu laughed. He shouted to the kitchen boys, who were below, already at Ling-Ten. "They are breaking ice for cooking water," he explained.

We headed down the nearly invisible path toward our new camp—and midday tea. Our tents lay in a peaceful green meadow, the first such green we had seen in over a week. We sprawled in the grass drinking tea and eating cheese and *chappattis*. George lay off to the side, reading a book. Jimmy and Boyd played a board game. Allen soon retired to his tent for a nap, while Jim talked with Anu and Dendi. I stretched out in the prickly grass, thinking about Anu and the other Sherpas who were with us. They were now our friends. It felt strange to have people do everything for us: cooking, helping to carry gear, setting up and breaking camp. Back in the United States, we were each used to doing these things for ourselves. Here, the Sherpas had not only helped us on the expedition, they had taught us about their customs, their religion, and their country. With little shared language, we had managed to become friends. I felt guilty sometimes because Anu, Dendi, Pasang, and the others earned very little money for their work. But in their society, the money was a lot and their jobs as guides gave them special status. This was the system in Nepal, so I would stick with it and be the best guest I knew how to be.

Afternoon fed into evening, and fog slithered up the valley until the tents were nearly invisible. We had had beautiful weather during this postmonsoon season. Trekking and climbing in Nepal takes place mostly during the spring and fall, before and after the monsoon. The monsoon is a period of rainstorms that sweep across southern Asia, drowning the land during late spring and summer. The monsoon brings enough rain for rice and other crops to grow. Sometimes, however, it causes flooding. If the storms arrive late and linger into the fall, high up in the mountains the rain turns to driving snow. This had happened earlier this fall when violent snowstorms raged across the Himalaya, causing avalanches and other disasters. Record numbers of people died in the mountains of Pakistan, India, and Nepal, including Julie Tullis, a world-famous mountaineer from England. Now, the weather was calm and kind, clear every day until the gentle afternoon fog rolled in. Buddha was watching over us.

"Hey! You always win," I heard Jimmy shout from behind the tent. Then I heard laughing. "The way this game is set up, there's no way I can win!" I walked around the side of the tent and leaned against a boulder, watching. Boyd just sat there grinning.

Later, at dinner, I was still thinking about the Sherpas. I asked Jim why Dawa and Purba, who were teenagers, weren't in school.

"Most students leave before completing high school," he explained. "They can obtain an SLC—School Leaving Certificate— by buying the answers to the exams from friends and others who have already taken them. The reasoning here is that you help a friend in any way you can because he's your friend. But that often means that a lot of students don't finish school."

After dinner I stood outside in the gray light of dusk. The evening fog had already lifted. I gazed up at the Kongma-La, a massive chute reaching more than eighteen thousand feet above the earth. Littered with scree, it loomed eerie and forbidding. Tomorrow we would have to tackle it. I shivered. The climbs were getting harder, and the nights colder.

MOUNTAIN METHODS

How to Find Your Route

When you travel in the mountains, you need to keep track of where you are and where you want to go. In addition to checking your map and compass, keep your eyes open to your surroundings. Try to remember landmarks such as a broken log, a fallen tree, or an unusual boulder. These may come in handy in helping you find your way.

Map

Carry a topographical map, one that shows trails and the type of terrain you will be climbing. You can get these from an outdoor-equipment shop, map store, or the local park service; or write to the United States Geological Survey (whose address is in "Getting Started" at the back of this book). Study your map before starting to climb. On topographical maps, the dotted lines are trails; thin wavy lines (called contour lines) tell you how steep the terrain is. Line up the map with landmarks near you, so that you can tell which direction you are headed. Always carry your map in a plastic bag to protect it from water.

Compass

Because your compass is a magnet, its arrow points to magnetic north, which is different from true north. (When you climb, you want to know in which direction true north lies.) The difference between true north and magnetic north is called the declination. Somewhere on your map you'll find a diagram that helps you determine true north on your compass. The diagram will be different for every map, so check this each time you climb.

Trail Markings

Most trails have markings to guide you. Some have blazes (painted marks) of a single color on trees and rocks along the way. Others are marked by cairns (piles of rocks). At trail junctions, there are usually signs telling you which trail is which and the distance to different destinations. Check your map each time you reach a trail junction.

Getting Lost

If you're lost, don't panic. Stop and look around you. Do you recognize any landmarks? Can you retrace your steps back to a familiar place? If not, stay put. Someone will find you.

11
Over the Kongma-La

IN THE STONE-COLD DARKNESS, Kancha whistled softly. I couldn't tell whether I was awake or asleep. Confused, I rolled over in my sleeping bag, pulling the edge up to my nose. I'd only slept for moments; suddenly it was morning. I sat up stiffly and reached for the tent zipper, gliding it open. Kancha squatted on his haunches with a pot of tea and the familiar cups dangling from his fingers.

"Bed tea, I know," I said groggily. "Thank you." He poured the tea, nodded, and left. I handed a cup to Boyd, who was just beginning to stir. The back of my throat ached from fatigue and the cold. I took careful sips, the warm liquid soothing the soreness. I didn't have the energy to get out my headlamp and look at my watch. I knew it was 4:00 A.M., and I knew it was below freezing outside the tent. I finished the tea and lay back down.

I cannot possibly climb an eighteen thousand-foot–high pass today, I thought. Only a day had passed since we had climbed Kala Pattar. Now we had to make our second, and final, warm-up climb. I rubbed my eyes, trying to psyche myself up. Then I propped myself on my elbows and struggled to a sitting position. I rummaged at the bottom of my sleeping bag for polypropylene socks, vapor-barrier socks (special plastic foot coverings for cold weather), and wool socks. Then I wriggled out of my down pants and into my now gritty wool hiking pants. I shoved my gear into my daypack and duffel and crawled out of the tent into the pale blue light of early morning. I headed to the cook tent, where Jim was waiting for all of us, curled up in a sleeping bag.

"Morning," I mumbled, settling on the floor of the tent. Boyd and Jimmy joined us. Allen and George still lay in their tents, asleep. Neither was feeling well. Today they would walk with the yaks and other staff down the valley, around the pass, and up the Imja Valley, meeting us in Chukhung for the night. I envied them this morning. I wanted to crawl back in my sleeping bag and never come out.

99

I downed another cup of tea, some runny porridge, and thick, doughy pancakes covered with honey. Then, stalling for as long as we could, we drank several more cups of tea. No one wanted to begin the climb. But finally, the time came and we moved out into the camp, hoisted our packs, and started up the long incline in the dark. Dendi led, the sound of his boots scuffling along in the pre-dawn gloom. Very quickly we separated along the steep route, each in his or her own world, trudging up the slope through yak dung and rubble.

Sleepy and light-headed, I relied on the climbing rhythm to carry me upward: breathe, breathe, step; breathe, breathe, step. I picked my way up the trail, zigzagging back and forth on the ever-steepening terrain. The high-pitched warble of a bird echoed off the walls of coal-black Mera Peak to the left. Somewhere, far away, I thought I heard the low rumble of an avalanche. But in between these bursts of sound, the ringing silence of the Himalaya persisted.

Time stretched to fill the distance we had to travel. I moved steadily, slowly pulling up and away from Jimmy and Boyd. Dendi leapt from rock to rock above me, his blue pack swaying, his feet sending a trickle of pebbles down the slope.

Gradually the slope seemed to give way, the ground becoming looser and less secure, changing from hard earth and rock to wobbling boulders, then to gravel. The sunrise was blocked by the ridge and walls of Kongma-La. Wind poured down the long funnel, slapping me in the face. Without sun, my muscles could not really warm up. It was as if the summit were scrambling to get away from us, making it harder and harder for us to reach it. Hour upon hour passed, and still no sun reached out to warm the pass. The ridge curved a dark outline above.

If I can only get up there, I thought, *I'll be in the sun.* I struggled upward to the lip of the ridge, triumphant. Immediately my heart sank.

It was the false summit. The true summit lay up and beyond this ridge. I could not manage to get warm, and my strength had been sapped from the start. A wedge of sun rested in the notch of the top of the pass, teasing me. The slope of scree and boulders streaming down from the notch was steeper and longer than any I had ever climbed. I stopped in my tracks.

Jimmy moved past me, silently. Wind echoed off the walls, billowing and curling down the chute like a long scarf. Dendi was way ahead. I looked down, behind me. Boyd was still far below. I was left to find the route alone, among the rocky debris. I trudged on, head down, arms and legs nearly rigid. I pushed air out of my lungs and allowed them to be filled again, like balloons. I kept my scarf wrapped around my neck and mouth to moisten the air I inhaled and reduce the sting of the wind. But the insides of my nostrils burned. I was climbing passively, expending as little energy as possible, trying to make it last the length of the incline. Wind spun through the pass, blowing me off balance, and I teetered backward over the long chute. The pass was too high, the gully too big, the slope too steep for me. This was how the Himalaya seemed, close up: too big. Tears of frustration burned my eyelids and I smeared them across my cheeks with my gloves. I was surely in a nightmare, running hard and not getting anywhere.

Boyd was still far below, beyond shouting distance. Up to my left, I spied a large overhang that might give me some protection from the wind while I rested. I made my way up to it and crawled in, my breath coming like a chugging locomotive. I rocked back and forth on my haunches. Then my heart and lungs began to quiet. I reached into my pack for a drink of water and a snack, and let my equilibrium return.

Then I stepped out onto the route again, my boots sinking ankle-deep in sandy scree, sliding backward. I fought back up to take another step and slid backward again. Cruel gusts battered my jacket and wind pants from every side. I dislodged some gravel, which slid down the slope toward Boyd, bouncing wildly, spraying out into the air. I spotted one cairn above me and worked my way toward it; then I followed the route to the next cairn and the next. The rocks were becoming larger again, and steadier. I looked up; the wedge of sunlight in the notch had grown wider and closer to me. A half a dozen more steps, and I was there. I clambered up onto a wide, flat rock and stood in the sun, letting the warmth sink in.

We have to work so hard for our pleasures here, I thought.

Jimmy and Dendi were just above me, waiting. When they saw me step into the sunlight, they waved. Jim, Boyd, Anu, and Nima came up and joined me. We were close to the true summit of the Kongma-La.

"Follow me," said Jim. "Learn to move with control, so that you can reverse any movement at will." He pressed each foot smoothly and deliberately into the rock, demonstrating that he could increase or decrease his speed at any moment. "Keep your hands at your sides. Don't use them on the rock because they'll throw you off balance rather than protect you." He walked along as if he were strolling down the sidewalk.

I followed Jim's example for several hundred feet. As we reached the snowline near the summit of the Kongma-La, Anu and Nima helped improve the trail by pushing loose boulders off the route and sending them tumbling down the chute. Nima picked up loose rocks and tossed them into space, laughing as they spun down out of sight. At snowline, there was a sudden chill and my boots sank into soft, sun-cupped snow. We crossed the snow patch, angling upward, and then we were there—on top of the Kongma-La, at 18,200 feet above sea level.

Perched on a narrow precipice, we gazed at the view on the other side, washed in sun. Then hunger attacked and we shared snacks of dried fruit, crackers, and popcorn, tossing the kernels into our mouths and gulping cold water to quench thirst.

"Who wants the marmite?" asked Jim, holding out the open jar of yeast spread.

"I do," I answered, and reached for the jar. I sank the blade of my pocketknife into the black, tarry goo and twirled it around, spreading the thick mess on a cracker. The tangy, salty snack broke in my mouth and stuck between my teeth. It was delicious.

We turned our attention back to the glorious mountains ahead of us, the new mountains that would surround us during our time in the Imja Valley. Directly above us was the magnificent southeast wall of Nuptse. In the distance were Makalu and Baruntse (Bar-uhn-tsay). Slightly below them stood Imja Tse (Im-jah tsay), the mountain we called Island Peak. Directly below us lay an unnamed lake, its massive blue-green ice riddled with cracks. I breathed deep with satisfaction. We could never see these mountains or this lake from a bus or a car; we had to walk to get here. Like lizards in the sun, we sat on the knife-edge of the Kongma-La a while longer, not thinking of the sheer drop directly below our boots, feeling the great joy of being in the Himalaya.

Eventually, we lifted our packs and brushed crumbs off our pants legs. Then we picked our way down the steep path to the trail leading to the valley. We skirted the lake and swung along, energized by the descent. We had done it: we had achieved our second shakedown climb. We still had a four-hour hike to Chukhung, but we were now on the march to our mountain.

The trail hugged the sides of the foothills of the great mountain. After a couple of hours, we stopped at the top of a monstrous fold in a hill, dropped our packs, and stretched out in the brown meadow for a rest. Nima pitched rocks down into the valley, and suddenly we heard clanking behind us: Dawa and Ang Purba sailed by, trotting on down the hill, pots and pans clanking in the baskets they carried on tumplines (leather straps) across their foreheads. Many Sherpas, and most of our kitchen boys, carried woven baskets filled with gear instead of backpacks. The strap across the forehead keeps the weight off the back, as high up as possible.

We watched as their loads bobbed down the hill, across the valley floor, and disappeared, blending in with the brown vegetation in the valley. Then we got up and followed them, switchbacking down the slope. At the bottom, Jimmy noticed an enormous boulder, forty feet high, hiding a cave.

"What great rockclimbing this would be!" he exclaimed. It was true. The smooth face of the boulder would be perfect for friction climbing, which means balancing weight and using the soles of the shoes to create friction that grips the rock. Cracks wandered up the side, providing hand jams and fingerholds. We explored further and stuck our heads into the cool entrance of the cave. You could even sleep here, protected from weather. But we moved on. We had a bigger mountain to climb.

We marched toward Island Peak, each lost in his or her own thoughts. When we reached another rock pile, Jimmy and Jim darted down it, flying from rock to rock. But I was beginning to tire. It seemed that each rock I stepped on tipped or wobbled. I looked at my watch. We had been on the trail for nearly twelve hours. I seem to have a limit: after twelve hours, everything seems the same. Gradually, I stumbled off the rock pile and onto the final hill leading down to the trail to Chukhung. I worked back and forth across the steep slant, dropping down onto the trail. I was weary, and I knew it.

The trail was interrupted by a shallow stream. I stopped and stared at it, confused. Water gushed fiercely over the rocks. I knew the others had crossed it; I just couldn't figure out how. Boyd came up behind me and leapt easily across, landing firmly on the other side. I just gazed at him blankly.

"You're hungry," he observed.

I shook my head in annoyance. "I'm not hungry at all. I'm just tired. I'm at my limit."

He came back across the stream and took my pack. "Follow me," he suggested.

"I can do it myself," I retorted angrily. But I wasn't so sure. I stumbled into the stream, my right boot sliding off a rock and splashing into the water. Furious, I pulled myself out of the brook.

"Here. Stop and eat something," Boyd said. He took out a granola bar and ripped off the wrapper. I took a bite. He was right. I was totally out of fuel. One of my problems with running out of fuel is that I begin to think I'm not hungry at all. I downed the granola bar and then ate a fruit bar, taking gulps of water in between. Afterward, I picked up my pack.

"Thanks. I'm OK now." But I was exhausted. I walked more steadily now, but without enthusiasm. Soon, we could see the low buildings of Chukhung, a yak-herding settlement, on the horizon. We arrived fifteen minutes later, to see Jim standing high on another hill outside the settlement, waving us up to our campsite.

I don't think I can make it, I thought. *I cannot climb another hill.*

I turned and forced my legs in the right direction, alternately perspiring and growing chilled. Clouds rolled up the valley and then pulled back as evening breezes blew in. I was filthy and tired, and all I wanted was to lie in a hot bubble bath and read a magazine. I thought I couldn't take another step.

But I did, shuffling up the last path through the glacial dust. Our campsite was a paradise: two large fields with views of Nuptse, Lhotse, Baruntse, and Ama Dablam. I collapsed inside the tent, peering out at the huge Nuptse wall, watching as the deep orange glow of final light faded into night.

MOUNTAIN METHODS
Climbing Rock

When you climb a mountain, you are bound to encounter rock—either on the trail in a nontechnical climb or as part of your route on a technical climb. If you plan to learn technical rockclimbing (climbing routes that require a rope and special techniques), take a course of instruction. For information, write to one of the organizations listed in "Getting Started" and ask if they offer a course near you; contact a local college outing club; check the YMCA or YWCA; or try an outdoor-gear shop. Use the following information as a springboard for your learning.

Nontechnical Rockclimbing

Plant your foot firmly on the rock, using your whole boot and keeping it level. If the trail goes up over a steep outcrop where you need to use your hands, move slowly and smoothly in order to keep your balance. Test footholds and handholds before putting your full weight on them. Make sure the rock is secure and won't flake off or fall away.

Technical Rockclimbing

Techniques

In a technical-rockclimbing course, you'll learn how to *belay,* or use your climbing rope to provide security for your climbing partner while he or she is climbing. You'll also learn how to *rappel,* or descend by sliding down the rope in a controlled manner. You'll learn how to use your hands and feet to grip, balance, and move your body up and down the rock. You'll even learn how to depend on your fingers with mere fingerholds!

Basic Equipment

Your course will teach you how to use the *climbing rope,* which is different from regular rope because it stretches so that it won't snap during a fall. You'll climb in a *harness,* which wraps around your waist and thighs and attaches to the rope. *Carabiners* (metal snap links) attach the harness to *ascenders* and *descenders.* Your instructor may require you to wear a *helmet,* which protects your head from injury if you fall and knock it against rock or if stones are dislodged by climbers above you. You may also wear rockclimbing shoes, which are designed to help you grip the rock and jam your feet into narrow areas.

12
A Yak-Herding Camp

ALTHOUGH PEOPLE DON'T live year round above seventeen thousand feet because the altitude can be harmful, some of the Sherpas in Nepal take their yaks to high-altitude camps such as Chukhung during the warmer parts of the year. When we arrived at Chukhung, it was nearly the end of the grazing season. Soon the yak drivers would take their herds back down to lower elevations. It was also near the end of the fall trekking and climbing season. Climbers still milled around, chatting in tea houses, comparing notes on mountains. We planned to spend a day camped at Chukhung, unpacking our climbing gear and checking to make sure everything was in good repair and that nothing was missing. Then we would repack our duffels, rearranging equipment for the climb. The following day we would head to Island Peak base camp.

At around 8:00 A.M., we set up a table in the sun and sat around it, savoring breakfast. I wolfed down pancakes smothered in honey, a bowl of porridge, two hard-boiled eggs, and several cups of tea.

Jim discussed the chores of the day. "We need to reorganize duffels for base camp and high camp. One duffel from each tent can go to high camp, one to base camp. Double up on spare items such as hats and mittens. Chances are, not everyone will need extras. Even double up on books—you can cut a novel in half and share it."

We discussed our route onto Island Peak and whether we should sleep on the glacier at high camp. It would mean sleeping on ice, but it would give us a head start toward the summit. George seemed to be feeling better; Allen complained that his stomach and the food weren't cooperating with each other.

The mood of the expedition had changed. For the past couple of weeks, we had been tourists learning about the culture of Nepal, enjoying the view of the mountains, and doing our shakedown climbs. Now all chores pointed to our climb of Island Peak.

After breakfast, we dragged out the contents of our tents. I asked Pasang to bring us a basin of hot water and collected dirty socks and long underwear to wash. I plunged my hands into the hot water, kneading the dirt out of the socks and long underwear. Dirt swirled around the wet clothes, clinging to them again as I lifted them out of the basin and wrung the gray water out of them, onto the ground. I slapped the clothes on a rock. Boyd strung a nylon cord from our tent to an ice ax staked in the ground and we hung the soaking, half-frozen clothes to dry in the sun. Nothing got very clean, but we felt as though it did.

I heard the padding of footsteps behind me and swung around. A Sherpani stood staring at me, wrapped in a black tunic with a red sweater pulled tightly across her shoulders. *"Namaste,"* I greeted her.

"Namaste," she nodded. Then she put her hands to both sides of her head. I stared at her, puzzled. She patted her temples with the palms of her hands. Suddenly, I got it. Her head hurt.

"Headache?" I asked. She nodded. "Wait here," I said and ducked inside the tent. I brought out two aspirin tablets and dropped them into her outstretched palm. She smiled slightly.

"Namaste," she said and shuffled away.

Anu gathered together the climbing Sherpas: Dendi, Nima, and Kancha. They would be scaling Island Peak with us. Pasang and the kitchen boys, along with Jettha and the yaks, would stay below at base camp. Anu instructed his Sherpas in how to prepare their climbing gear for Island Peak. They yanked on their hiking boots, adjusted crampons, measured ropes, and fashioned rope harnesses. Pasang sat to the side, watching. The Sherpas are given bonuses with which to outfit themselves with climbing gear so they obtain the equipment as cheaply as possible and keep the change. They may borrow equipment from a friend or relative or purchase it from another Sherpa. As a result, the gear isn't always the best or even in very good condition.

Jim saw us watching them. "Sometimes you'll see the Sherpas running around the mountain unroped. They also often use poor equipment instead of good equipment. I can't enforce the same standards on them—though sometimes I have to draw the line for safety. I have seen some of them use baling twine for crampon straps. We give them money for gear, but they pocket most of it. If Anu's brother in Chukhung owns an ice ax and uses it only three times a year, it's cheaper for Anu to rent that ice ax from his brother than to buy a new or better one."

Anu, Kancha, Dendi, and Nima check climbing gear at Chukhung. Pasang, in the white hat, watches.

We arranged our own climbing gear on the orange drop cloth we usually used when we ate on the ground. We checked our boots and strapped the crampons to the boots, adjusting them. Next we rifled through carabiners and harnesses and identified our helmets. We had already collected our ice axes and were carrying them strapped to our daypacks. Now we would add the rest of the climbing gear to our packs in order to get used to carrying the weight on the final climb.

I returned to our tent and stripped the gear in my duffel to the bare essentials. We could take sleeping bags and pads, climbing hardware, a small first-aid kit, snacks, headlamp, and extra socks. I yanked the dense flannel liners out of my rubber camp boots—I'd sleep in them when it got really cold. We'd be sleeping and climbing in the same clothes for a couple of days; there would be no chance to change. But I cheated and threw in my down pants to wear at high camp; I knew I'd be cold.

By late morning I emerged into the sun again, stumbling slightly as I walked to the meal tent for lunch. Although I didn't feel sick or dizzy at this altitude, the slightest chore left me short of breath.

We ate lunch outdoors at the wobbly table. We worked our way through thick slices of tough, flavorful yak steak with green beans and greasy french fries. Yak steak was always delicious to me. Cooked this way, it reminded me of spare ribs. Smoke from the dung fire that boiled the water drifted from the kitchen tent out around the table. Yaks wandered along the surrounding hills, their bells clanging in the distance.

"Pass the fries, Al-tee-tude," commanded Boyd. Allen sent the greasy tin down the table. Allen's new nickname stuck.

After lunch, George went off on a hike by himself, striding up into the hills. We finished packing, lay in the sun, read books, took a short walk, and played board games. This was our last chance to rest before the long journey up the mountain.

The sun dipped toward the horizon as bitter cold crept up through the glacier valley. The colder it got, the more I fantasized about home. As I scribbled in my diary, the ink dried and froze. I longed for one of the plush, warm sweaters in my bureau at home. I wanted steaming, rich cocoa that I could drink for its flavor rather than the few seconds of warmth it gave me.

I walked to the meal tent, where Boyd and Jimmy played back-gammon in the flickering candlelight. Clouds of breath puffed from their mouths as they made deliberate, nearly frozen moves with fingerless gloves. Bundled in their heavy expedition parkas, they looked like an advertisement for outdoor gear. It was now pitch dark and George still had not returned from his hike. Jim stuck his head in the tent.

"Has anyone seen George?" he asked. We shook our heads. Jim headed to the Sherpas' kitchen tent to make arrangements to search for George.

Two Sherpas arrived in camp, having heard that someone was missing. They said they had seen a "tall guy, blue pack" a while back, on the ridge above camp. Jim ran outside and called George's name, his voice echoing up and down the valley. Jim then returned to the tent and discussed a search with Anu and Kancha. As they hoisted their packs and flicked on flashlights, George wandered into camp.

"I overshot camp several times," he explained, looking relieved. "Eventually, I ran into two Sherpas. They had heard me calling Jim and Anu and they knew our camp."

We sat on our wobbly stools inside the meal tent, this night eating at the table instead of crouching on the ground. Dawa came in with huge pots filled with *momos* and sauce, his sleeves rolled up to hide the rips in his shirt. His teeth chattered and he shivered as he placed the heavy pot on the table.

I've got to find something for him to wear, I thought. It was only about fifteen degrees outside and he had no sweater or coat. I shuddered in my own down parka, pile jacket, sweater, and down pants.

We passed around meat *momos,* slurped down warm broth, and devoured sugary Jell-O, discussing our climbing strategy on the mountain. We decided to skip the extra day of climbing practice that we had allowed ourselves in order to make a fast stab at the summit if the weather was good. That way, if we had bad weather, we could try again. Jim reviewed some of the strategies that he had found most useful in the Himalaya.

"Often in the Himalaya, the safest action is the fastest action. We don't always follow the practices here that we might in the Alps or in the Rockies back home. If we have a group of six and one member falls into a crevasse (a large crack in the ice), the best thing is to pull him—or her—out as fast as possible and not wait around to set up a complicated pullup. Island Peak, even though it isn't as high as Everest or Nuptse, is a big mountain. Complicated processes take a long time, including getting help. So the best thing is to move fast."

Purba came in with pots of boiled water and filled our water bottles. We would stuff these at the foot of our sleeping bags to keep us warm and to keep the water—which was tomorrow's drinking water—from freezing. From drinking to washing to the comfort of warmth, water was vital to every aspect of the expedition. We couldn't do without it.

Back in the tent, I settled in for the night, lying in the frozen stillness as yak bells brushed close to the walls of the tent and heavy hooves pawed the dirt.

MOUNTAIN METHODS

Water

If you had to go without food for days or even weeks, you could survive. But you can't survive nearly that long without water. When you hike and climb mountains, you must carry water. If you plan to stay overnight, you may need to add to your water supply from another source.

How Much Water?

When you climb, you lose a lot of water in one day from sweat, breathing, and urination. You need to replace that water, even if you don't feel thirsty. Keeping your body filled with the right amount of water will help it function properly, including helping your muscles work. On a day trip, whether in winter or summer, carry at least two one-liter plastic bottles filled with water. Finish them both by the end of the day. As you gain experience, you may discover you need more, but you won't need less. If you plan to stay overnight, carry one or two extra bottles. (You'll need water for cooking and washing, as well as extra drinking water.)

Clean Water

If you need to add to your water supply, use water from a running stream. Don't take water from a stagnant pond. Even the coldest, clearest stream is bound to contain bacteria and pollution, so it's important to clean the water, or purify it. The easiest way to do this is by using iodine tablets that you drop in your water bottle. (You can buy these at a drugstore or outdoor-gear shop.) Or you can boil the water for twenty minutes at your camp. There are also special filters you can buy at outdoor-gear shops. Drinking polluted water can cause illnesses. (One of these is giardia, but its symptoms—vomiting, diarrhea, and stomach cramps—may not appear for a week or two.)

Dehydration

When your body doesn't get enough water, it becomes dehydrated. If you are dehydrated, you may notice a headache. You probably won't urinate very often, and when you do, the urine will be a dark yellow color. Vomiting and diarrhea cause dehydration, so if you develop one of these conditions, try to drink as much water as you can.

13
Toward Island Peak

As WE SLEPT, a strong night wind pounded the camp. It battered the tent and tore at the tent ropes. When I emerged for breakfast in gray light, dust whipped at my cheeks and mouth. We scrunched into the meal tent. Today we could not eat outside. I looked at the bowl of hard-boiled eggs and sticky porridge without enthusiasm.

"When I get home, my first meal is going to be lasagna, spinach salad, and pumpkin pie," I announced, cracking a hard-boiled egg against my plastic cereal bowl.

"I'd just like more noodles," said Allen. I glared at him. If I ate one more bowl of noodles, I was going to be sick.

"I'll eat everything off our farm—beef, ham, you name it," piped in Jimmy.

Slowly I peeled the egg, dipped the end into a patch of salt, and bit into the cool, jiggly white of the egg. I chewed methodically, swallowed, and then dug into the glob of porridge growing cold in the bowl. I was hungry all the time, but I was tired of the same old food. I couldn't seem to eat enough—but sometimes I couldn't take another bite of noodles, greasy potatoes, or gloppy porridge. But I hadn't come on this trip for the food. And Pasang was doing the best he could. It wasn't his fault. It was hard to carry supplies for many miles over rough terrain. Besides, there weren't many chances to buy fresh groceries, except potatoes and a chicken here and there. So eating became a chore. We kept ourselves stuffed because we needed all the energy we could get.

Dendi and Kancha broke camp in a torrent of wind, the nylon tents billowing up in the air. We each grabbed a corner of a tent and held it down so it could be rolled tight and tied to the yaks.

I pulled my anorak over my head, added a wool cap, and drew my hood up, tightening the strings. Then I wound my scarf tightly around my nose and mouth and zipped gaiters around my calves to

keep the dust out of my boots. By the time I slipped on red polypropylene gloves, I felt like a mummy.

We set out among violent gusts along the moraine toward Island
Peak base camp. The altitude had left me weak and wobbly, and I
was buffetted around as I struggled along the trail. I could barely
see a few feet ahead, through the blowing dust. Powdery grit from
the glacier swirled around my legs and up into my face, shooting
behind my sunglasses and lodging in the corners of my eyes and
eyelashes. I coughed constantly, pulling my scarf tighter around
my mouth, feeling the wool moisten with my breath.

Dust hung in the air in clouds, drifting across the valley. Ahead,
the mountains stood behind a beige veil. The trail dipped east.
After a couple of hours, we found a fairly calm spot to rest, crawling behind rocks and beneath scrubby bushes. As we sat in the
scrub, the branches crumbled and more dust puffed around our
faces.

"You're glistening!" exclaimed Jimmy when he turned to me. I
looked down at my blue anorak. It was coated in sparkling dust—
powdery mica from the glacier.

Boyd gazes at Island Peak, on the approach walk.

I unzipped my pack and took out my water bottle, trying to keep the water free from dirt. As I gulped it down, the cold liquid soothed my parched throat. I passed the bottle to Boyd. We sat gazing across the wide, flat expanse bleached colorless by the sun. It was like a vast desert, at seventeen thousand feet above sea level; and we had to cross it. We stood, shouldered our packs, and started down into the ocean of dust and sand.

Beaten back by wind and choking dust, we headed up the Imja Valley. The roar of the wind was so great that our shouts were slapped back in our own faces. In the distance, a line of trekkers shimmered like a mirage. An hour passed, and they grew a little closer. A half hour later, we greeted them halfway across the expanse where an empty tumble-down stone hut stood exposed to the sand and wind. Their bright red anoraks sparkled with mica dust. They were Swiss climbers who had scaled Island Peak the day before. Eagerly, we asked them questions. One of the men knew a little English.

"Very windy," was his report of the mountain. I thought back to the beginning of our trip, all the way to Kathmandu. We had been delayed two days because of fog at the airport. If we had been on our original schedule, we would have attempted the summit of Island Peak today. We never would have made it in this wind. I gazed around at the weird, barren landscape. Buddha was surely watching over us.

We left the Swiss climbers to their lunch of canned sardines and continued our march across the parched river valley. Finally, the trail angled up among some boulders. It was a relief just to have something different to look at and walk on. After a while, the trail rounded a corner and there stood a small stone enclosure. Pasang was sitting in the yard. Dendi and Dawa scurried about. They looked up as we approached and waved us into the yard.

"Lunch," said Kancha, coming out of the dark enclosure. Dust wafted up from our boots as we kicked them off and we padded across the orange plastic tarp that followed us everywhere. I crouched and sat cross-legged up against the stone wall, as low as possible to stay out of the wind. Purba appeared with a tray of food: baked beans, tuna, *chappattis* with marmite, and tea. I waved off his offer of the hot, sweet orange drink; I could not drink it anymore. Within seconds, a soft grit had settled on the food. We shoveled down lunch as quickly as possible in an effort to keep the dirt out of our mouths. But dust settled everywhere—on the cold utensils, on our clothes, on Allen's uneaten scoop of beans.

After the Swiss climber's report, we had begun to think of the weather and conditions on the mountain. We discussed this during lunch. We couldn't climb on a day such as this; the wall was too exposed and the summit ridge too narrow. Gusts could send someone sailing off the ridge and a thousand feet down through space before landing. Fighting wind all the way would sap our strength and make any technical maneuvers difficult. But neither did we want fog or snow. Each of us gazed at the sky and hoped for the ideal day.

After lunch, I got up and strolled outside the enclosure, leaning against an enormous boulder. Ahead, Island Peak stood behind a yellow haze. Though dwarfed by Lhotse next to it, it was still a big mountain. The snow wall was a large white wedge banded by a greenish-blue glacier on either side. I strained to see climbers, knowing that I really couldn't—it was still too far away. Snow swirled off the summit in a long, white plume.

In just two days, if all goes well, we'll be there, I thought. *We'll be on top, looking down instead of up.*

Jimmy offered me a stale, soft Lifesaver from a pack he'd bought somewhere along the trail. I bit into the chewy, tart candy and its stickiness spread across my tongue. Then he came back with a package of stale bubblegum.

"Where'd you get this stuff?" I asked, laughing.

"Namche," he replied. "I couldn't pass it up." I took a piece and peeled off the wrapper, popping the pink square in my mouth. It was rock-hard. I turned it over and over with my tongue. My teeth just couldn't sink in. Finally, I held it in the back of my mouth behind a molar. The sugary flavor seeped through my mouth, keeping it moist at least.

We packed up and took off along the moraine again. As I started up quickly, I felt as though helium instead of blood were flowing through my veins. I could have floated right up into the sky. I couldn't tell how fast I was moving, but I wobbled along, feeling silly and light-headed, apparently making progress. Still, the big mountains seemed just as far away as they had this morning.

The altitude continued to press down on Boyd as he trudged along, one painful step at a time. "I feel as though I'm pulling an entire train," he said, but he didn't complain beyond that.

The trail dropped down again to another wide, sandy valley, and we began to circle the base of Island Peak. Nuptse and Lhotse lay to our left. Baruntse, 23,390 feet high, loomed dead ahead. We would see three sides of Island Peak by the time we finished the climb from the southeast side. Wind gusted across the gray glittering sand, searing through all protection. Creeping toward the massive Baruntse wall, I felt like an ant crawling toward an anthill. Then gradually, rocks began to litter the sand and we were picking our way through them, my floppy ankles not cooperating very well. We ducked behind a few large boulders for bathroom stops and then took pictures of the huge mountains rising above the giant valley. Dendi led us now, his lantern swinging from one hand, his leather-covered portable radio slung over his shoulder. High, tinny strains of Indian music pierced the air as we walked. Finally, we walked up a hill and rounded a corner. There lay base camp.

In a wild tumble of rocks, Nima and Kancha had pitched the tents as even and level as they could. We stashed our daypacks and wandered around. Only one other party was here, although there were plenty of signs of past expeditions. As at Lobuche, trash was strewn everywhere. Jim handed wicker baskets to Nima and Kancha—one basket for burnable trash and the other for garbage that couldn't be burned. Soon we were picking through yak dung for rusty cans, toilet paper, limp plastic wrappers from noodles, soft, used tea bags, even a set of chopsticks. I turned over rocks and found more trash crushed into the ground. We filled the baskets within a few minutes, but we couldn't carry out everyone else's litter. We still had a mountain to climb and another week's walk back to Lukla. The Nepalese were sometimes amused at our efforts to get rid of other people's trash. But it was quite clear that while they tolerated their own trash, they didn't want to put up with garbage from others. We started a small fire in a charred pit that someone had used for cooking and burned what we could. Smoke mingled with the dust and the camp smelled sharp and sour.

I crawled into the tent before dinner to try to clean up. Dirt had already worked itself inside the tent. It was ground into my wool pants and pile jacket as well as my ears and nose. Every time we opened the tent flap, a gale of grit blew in and settled on the sleeping bags and duffels.

"Hey, I'm covered with fairy dust!" Jimmy shouted from his

tent. I found myself looking forward to tomorrow night, when we would sleep on nice, clean ice.

At 5:00 P.M., Dawa stood outside. "Hello, soup ready," he announced. As I followed him to the meal tent, I looked down at myself. I was now going to dinner swaddled in wool pants, down coverall pants, a turtleneck, sweater, pile jacket, parka, hat, gloves, and felt-lined camp boots. I was also sleeping and hiking in the same clothes—partly to reduce the weight we carried, but also because I thought that if I didn't go through the motions of a daily change, the climb would come faster and the hardships would be over sooner.

Camp was quiet. The Japanese climbers with whom we shared base camp squatted next to a fire. We were lucky to have so few people here. But down at Tengboche, this was the week of Mani Rimdu, a popular celebration for trekkers and climbers to attend. So it looked like we'd have Island Peak nearly to ourselves.

I crouched inside the kitchen tent. Immediately my stomach cramped. I had daily stomach aches now from hunching over too often in our own tent and at meals. We had only used a table a few times on the trail. I longed to sit in a chair to read, to sit at a table to eat. As we passed around bowls of noodle soup, Jim threatened to open a restaurant when we got back home. He'd call it "Tastes of Trekking" and serve dry *chappattis* with marmite, cold omelets, and tough yak steak. Guests must change their money at the door for rupees. And a fan would blow dirt and yak dung around the room.

Back in the tent for the night, I snuggled down into my sleeping bag as the yaks ambled through camp, their hooves clacking against rocks. Tomorrow, we would leave them behind, along with Jettha, Pasang, and the kitchen crew. We would carry only the bare necessities, accompanied by Anu, Dendi, Nima, and Kancha. Tomorrow night, we would be on the ice below the giant Island Peak wall. The day after would be a day of truth for us all. The faraway rumble of an avalanche echoed through the night. Then there was silence.

MOUNTAIN METHODS

Weather

When you climb a mountain, you can't escape the weather. Weather affects how far you can see, how warm or cold you are, and how slippery or firm the ground is. In extreme situations, weather may even threaten your life. You need to be prepared for anything and learn how to read the signs of weather.

1. *Be prepared.* Even if the sky is brilliant blue, and it is warm and sunny at the foot of the mountain, be prepared for wind, rain, and snow on top. Always carry rain gear that covers you and your pack. Take a windbreaker, extra socks, a hat, and gloves even if you are hiking in warm weather. You may have an unplanned overnight stay on the mountain.

2. *Read the signs.* As you hike, check the sky often for signs that may tell you bad weather is approaching. Streaky clouds that blend into a blanket, a fuzzy ring around the sun or moon, or a cloud hiding the summit of the mountain and continuing to grow can all mean rain or snow is on its way. In the southwest, where mountains rise above deserts, huge clouds that turn dark gray or purple usually mean a storm is coming. Also, if the wind kicks up or changes direction, bad weather may follow. Some people say they can "smell" a storm on its way; if the air suddenly turns clear and has a fresh smell, rain may be coming.

3. *If you get caught in a storm.* If it begins to rain or snow, stop and put on your rain gear right away, covering your pack. If you are above treeline, get back down into the forest if possible so that you are not a target for lightning, and to help avoid hypothermia. Stay

away from rock overhangs; they attract lightning. If you have crampons or an ice ax, place them at least several feet away from yourself. Try to walk slowly so you don't overheat and drench the inside of your rain gear with sweat; otherwise, you will become chilled later. If you need to set up camp, raise your tent first; then crawl in and take off your wet clothes, putting on dry ones. If it's snowing, shake the snow off your boots and parka before entering the tent.

14
Carry to High Camp

AT DAWN, the Sherpas gathered juniper branches and lit them on fire, the sweet smoke curling through camp. The burning branches were meant to wish us good fortune on our climb. They chanted the Buddhist prayer, *Om mani padme hum* (Hail the jewel in the lotus) for our safety. (The lotus is a type of plant about which many stories have been told.) The climbing of a mountain is very serious for the Sherpas, for local gods are said to live on the summits of mountains. In addition to Buddha, the Sherpas believe in smaller gods that protect Sherpa villages and farms. Some mountains, such as Khumbila (Koom-bee-lah) near Namche Bazaar, are named after the gods who live on them.

So we were climbing to the home of the Sherpa gods. Nima, Kancha, Dendi, and Anu would accompany us. But for each Sherpa, the decision whether or not to climb all the way to the summit is very personal. Some Sherpas choose to climb most of the mountain, stopping just short of the summit. Tomorrow, we would see who among our Sherpas would go to the top.

In the dining tent, we ate hard-boiled eggs, porridge, and Pasang's lightest pancakes yet as if they were our last meal. Outside, the Sherpas continued to chant their prayers. Jettha whistled for the yaks, who had wandered up the hill.

After breakfast, Anu and Dendi headed off first, loaded down with heavy packs, climbing hardware dangling from the sides. By the end of the day, Dendi would have made two full trips, all the way up to high camp and back, then up to high camp again with a second load. I stood outside the meal tent, watching them walk off among the rocks in the cold, grim morning. I bent and fumbled with nylon straps, lashing my crampons, ice ax, and camera to the outside of my pack. I crammed my expedition parka into a yellow stuff-sack and attached it to the outside of the pack with stretching cords. Then I swung the heavy pack, which had my plastic mountaineering boots in it, onto my shoulders and adjusted it, breathing hard. My fingers and toes were rigid with cold. I bounced back and forth from foot to foot, trying to warm up. Then I turned and walked briskly up the valley, leaning toward the sun that lay ahead.

By now, I wanted to get to the top of Island Peak—to get the job done. One of the hardships of climbing in the Himalaya is that it takes so long to get to the mountain you plan to climb. You can't drive to it or take a train or bus as you might to the Rockies or the Alps. You must walk for a week, sometimes several weeks, to get to the base of the mountain. By then, everyone in the party has had some kind of illness—sore throat, altitude sickness, diarrhea—and is feeling weak. There is always the altitude to deal with—where the rest of the world's mountains end, the Himalaya begin. When you are ready to climb the mountain, chances are you are already exhausted.

Boyd followed me, slowly, painfully. The altitude had completely drained him of strength and his pale, weary face showed beneath the red stubble of beard. By the time we reached the steep slope leading to the base of Island Peak, Kancha had caught up and taken Boyd's pack, stacking it above his own, across his neck. Boyd trudged along in his bright green parka and red ski cap, head down, his gloved hands in his pockets.

I labored up the hill, breathing short, hollow breaths, hacking a sharp cough that had settled so deeply in my chest that my stomach hurt every time I coughed.

The incline was now so steep that my ankles burned with the effort of keeping my boots upright, clinging to the dirt. I made switchbacks to alternate the weight on my ankles, but soon the pain in the uphill and downhill ankles grew equal, spreading up into my calves. Then the hard ground gave way to loose rock and scree. The altitude hit me suddenly and I swayed and stopped. I could barely lift my feet off the ground and so made little stumbling, shuffling movements. Adrenaline shot through my system; then I was out of breath again. Boyd had fallen farther and farther behind and I agonized with his every step.

I must keep going, I said to myself, *or I'll never make it.*

Finally I had to stop. I could walk no farther. I fumbled around in the pouch of my anorak and found a cherry cough drop, popping it in my mouth. Then I drank some water, letting the coolness flow over the tart cherry on my tongue. Kancha and Boyd trudged up behind me. They waved me on, wordlessly. The sun baked the ground, my wool pants, and my anorak. The sky was brilliant and harsh; the surrounding mountains were growing closer. The Imja Valley fell farther and farther away. We did not have energy or breath for conversation. I grew annoyed at Kancha and Boyd for expecting me to find the route among the confusing mess of loose shale and rock. Every handhold I grabbed at pulled free; every rock I stepped on wobbled, and I swayed out over nothing. I was losing strength fast. Finally, I turned to Kancha as I had on Kala Pattar.

"Can you lead?" I asked. He understood immediately and stepped ahead, up onto an outcrop. Then he turned around, leaned down, and offered me his hand. I took it gratefully, and he guided me up with ease. My confidence returned. I stopped to pour some dried fruit pieces down my throat, but the relief was short-lived. As if the route were not already hard enough, above us it grew even steeper. With the altitude, I lost my balance even more often and imagined myself spinning off into the air, plummeting down to the valley below. Then I spotted the tiny bright dots that were the hats of Jim, Jimmy, George, Allen, Anu, and Nima bobbing above the ridge at snowline, where they had stopped to put on their climbing boots and crampons.

I hit snowline and hauled myself onto the pinnacle where the others were perched, hastily strapping on crampons. We were now at nearly nineteen thousand feet, higher than we had ever been— above Kala Pattar and the Kongma-La.

I found a small patch of snow among the rocks and let go of my pack. Less than three feet from me the cliff dropped two thousand feet to the glacier valley below. We sat almost level with the blue-green Imja Glacier, which hung precariously off the mountain, as if it had stopped suddenly in midair. In the distance, I could barely see the figures of two climbers from another party, making their way down from the summit of Island Peak.

Boyd joined me and we began the chore of removing our hiking boots, pulling on plastic mountaineering boots, strapping on crampons, and untying our ice axes from our packs. Careful not to drop anything, I shoved my dusty hiking boots into the bottom of my pack. I stood up, teetering on the crampons. Then I picked my way over and around the rocks, my feet sliding and catching on the stone, until I reached the ridge of bright, hard, solid snow leading to high camp.

This is it, this is what we came for, I thought, as my crampons crunched over the snow and my ice ax sliced through the crust. Higher than I'd ever gone before, on a brilliant day in the clean air and crisp snow—high above the dust, dirt, yak dung, smoky fires—this was paradise. I stopped for a moment and looked around. Behind me, the jagged rock ridge curved down and out of sight like the tail of a dragon. The giant snow wall of Baruntse stood coldly supreme in the midday sun. On all sides, peaks split the sky. And ahead lay our mountain: Island Peak.

We arrived at high camp at about 1:00 in the afternoon. Anu, Jim, and Dendi had bolted ahead and had laid out the bright green tents and the orange cook tent in the snow. I wandered around aimlessly, befuddled due to the altitude and fatigue. Gradually, each of us plopped down on the nearest duffel, backpack, or odd piece of equipment. My head pounded hard behind my eyeballs. I reached for my water bottle and tried to drink, but could take only sips because gulps left me breathless. Anu, Nima, and Dendi rushed around camp getting everything ready for a night on snow and ice. I felt guilty just sitting and watching them, but I felt as though I couldn't move. My feet and legs were too heavy and my head was too light. Eventually, I stood and helped the others pound the snow into hard, flat platforms for the tents. Then we unfolded the tents, shaking them out. We drove stakes into the ice and packed more snow around them to keep them secure during the night. Luckily, there was no wind, for the tents could be blown right off the ledge. Jim dug a square hole behind one of the tents to use as a latrine. The chill was painful while hovering over the hole, but the view of Makalu made up for it.

At about 3:00, with our home base established, Jim, Anu, and Nima set off to set fixed lines on the snow wall for the next day's climb. Laden with ropes, carabiners, and ice screws, they marched up the smooth white slope toward the sun while the rest of us lounged around in our tents or in the last of the light. I hoped desperately for good weather the next day.

I have only one day of climbing left in me, I thought.

Before dinner, Kancha passed around a tin pot of *makai* that tasted like kerosene. The kerosene stove hissed from inside the Sherpas' orange tent.

Jim, Anu, and Nima returned. Jim popped a few puffs of *makai* in his mouth. "Last spring, when I brought another group to

Gear is strewn everywhere as we set up high camp at nineteen thousand feet above sea level. Jim, in the foreground, directs operations.

Island Peak, I was the last one off the mountain, coming down to the final ridge where the snow turns to rock. I was carrying two ropes and my pack was heavy. I tripped—it was as if my feet were tied together—and fell, rolling over twice down the icy slope before I stopped. When I got up, my head was bleeding everywhere in the snow. The cut wasn't bad, but a concussion could have been serious at altitude. And no one would have thought to come back for me for a long time. It just brought home to me again how easy it is to make a slip at the end of the day, when you're tired."

Kerosene fumes drifted out of the cook tent, and we moved to Jim, George, and Allen's sleep tent, which for tonight would be our meal tent. There, we huddled over a large pot of noodles, a small dish of curry, and warm canned fruit. Darkness settled outside around the tiny tents perched on the edge of an ice cliff. We tried to talk about everything except the climb.

Finally, Jim said, "Let's get some sleep. Breakfast at 4:00 A.M. tomorrow."

To save weight and space, we had only brought two sleeping tents, so Jimmy squeezed into the other narrow tent with us. We

took turns wriggling into our sleeping bags like three giant cater-
pillars in soft cocoons. Our breath puffed white in the cold air, its
dampness settling on the outside of our sleeping bags and forming
crystals on the walls of the tent. We changed our socks and rolled
our warm water bottles down to the ends of our sleeping bags. We
shut off our headlamps and lay there in silence, each wide awake.
My breath began to come in short gasps and I sat up, in a panic.

"Are you OK?" asked Jimmy.

"Sure," I answered, and slowly my breath quieted. Altitude often affects your breathing patterns when you lie down and even
when you sleep.

Boyd and Jimmy soon fell asleep and I lay awake, marveling at
being on a glacier at nineteen thousand feet above sea level, a long
way from home. I shivered and reached for a cherry cough drop,
thinking about the mountain. I closed my eyes just to keep my
eyeballs warm as the long, cold night reached out to me like a dark
arm, beckoning.

MOUNTAIN METHODS

Winter Hiking and Camping

Hiking and camping in winter have their own special challenge and thrill. The weather may be harsh and cold, but the snowy mountains are beautiful and quiet. Your goal on a winter trip is to stay warm and dry, preventing frostbite and hypothermia. You should be an experienced warm-weather climber before you try climbing in winter. In addition to the information that follows, be sure to read all the other "Mountain Methods" in this book. If possible, take a winter-hiking course.

Planning a Winter Trip

As you plan your trip, remember that climbing takes longer in winter than in summer. Snow and ice, along with heavy clothing, make the going slower and more difficult. Trail markers may be covered with snow. Breaking trail and crossing streams also take a long time. Before going on your trip, practice strapping on crampons and snowshoes as well as setting up the tent and stove with gloves on at home. For day trips, always set a turnaround time—the time when you'll turn around to get back to shelter or home before dark.

Climbing the Mountain

Read "Mountain Methods: Climbing Snow and Ice" following chapter 15. On a nontechnical climb, you'll need crampons when the trail becomes steep and snowshoes when the snow becomes so deep that your boots sink down into it. A technique for descending a snow slope is called "glissading," which is a controlled slide. You'll learn this skill in a winter-hiking or winter-climbing course.

Camping

Before dark, choose a level spot. Then stamp down the snow and put up your tent. Start your stove, then gather snow to melt right away. After dinner, hang your food in trees (except a small snack to keep in the tent). You may want to fill your water bottles with hot water, then bury them in your sleeping bag to keep them from freezing. Check them for leaks first! Once inside your tent, remove all your wet clothing and replace it with dry clothes. If you wake up in the middle of the night, eat your snack; the calories will help keep you warm.

15
"Slowly, Slowly Is Best"

I DO NOT KNOW whether I slept. The sharp beep of Boyd's watch alarm pulsed through the silence. I rolled over in my sleeping bag and tugged my ski cap down over my ears. I'd worn most of my clothes all night but I was still chilled. Boyd pulled on his headlamp and soft circles of light slid along the tent wall and down the sleeping bags. He checked the thermometer: zero degrees. I shivered. The harsh cold crept over my face. Jimmy rolled over.

"Morning!" he said, cheerfully. It was 3:00. No bed tea this morning. We had to save water and time. As I lay in my sleeping bag, breathing became difficult. At high altitude, it is harder to lie down than to sit up. So I sat up—slowly. Cold air rushed through the opening of my sleeping bag. I pulled the ends of the bag up around my shoulders. My hands were dry and blue from the cold. I brushed my hair and began to put on still more clothes from the bottom of my sleeping bag. We were so cramped inside the tent that Jimmy, Boyd, and I took turns moving around.

We collected our gear, stuffed the frozen sleeping bags into frozen nylon sacks, and crept out onto the hard snow. The sky was black and the snow bright white and crunchy. We each crawled into Jim, Allen, and George's tent for breakfast. Hunched over, stiff with heavy, bulky clothing, I tried to sit cross-legged. My stomach muscles cramped. I tried to smile. Kancha appeared with a steaming pot of hot water.

"Tea!" he cried softly in the dark. He reached in through the tent flaps and poured steaming water into the cold plastic cups. We drank quickly before the water could cool off. Then we passed around corn flakes, sliding them into plastic bowls. Kancha reappeared. "*Dudh!*" he called this time, and poured hot, thin milk on each bowl of corn flakes. I bolted it down too, trying to get as much warmth in me as possible. Then Jim ripped open a bag of M&Ms, dropping a few into each of our hands.

"We need to talk about ropes," he began. "There are six of us, and four climbing Sherpas—Anu, Dendi, Kancha, and Nima Kancha. We'll need two ropes of three. Kancha will rope up with two of you, and the other three will rope together. I'll be on my own, with Anu, Dendi, and Nima Kancha."

"Boyd and I will be slower than the other guys," I volunteered. "So I think we should rope up with Kancha." Everyone nodded. The matter was settled. We moved slowly, one by one, out into the dark again, to put on climbing gear. Headlamps flashed over the snow, climbing packs, and the tents. I pulled on stiff, crackly Gore-tex climbing pants. Then I sat on a pack and tried to yank on the frozen plastic mountaineering boots. Even though I had kept them inside the tent, under the foot of my sleeping bag to maximize warmth, they were like ice. I jammed in my right foot. Instantly cold spread along the bottom of my foot; it was aching within a matter of seconds. Then I bent down and jammed in my second foot. I untangled my climbing harness and stepped into it clumsily. I checked my jumar ascender (the metal handle attached by a cord to my harness), which I would clip to the main climbing rope. I also checked my carabiners, the oblong metal clips that fastened the jumar cord to my harness. Then I crouched to put on crampons. Suddenly, I began to shiver. I was so cold I was near tears. I could not let the rest of the team see me this way. I couldn't think straight; I understood that my core temperature was probably beginning to drop—a sign of hypothermia. Boyd, working on his gear next to me, noticed. He dropped what he was doing and crouched in front of me, stripping off his mittens.

"Here, let me help you with the crampons." Gratefully, I let him take hold of my boot. He tugged the straps tight and buckled them around my boot. Then he blew on his hands to warm them and yanked the strap to the other crampon tight.

"I'm so cold that I'm scared," I said quietly. Without a word, he took my pack and made sure everything necessary was in it: water, food, and extra clothing. I felt embarrassed; then guilt swept through me. I knew that if I could bear the cold until the sun came up, I would be fine; I would make the summit. I had acclimatized well at nineteen thousand feet and I knew I could climb the last thousand feet to the top of Island Peak. I wasn't so sure about Boyd; he still hadn't been able to acclimatize.

Coils of rope lay in the snow and we each clipped to our assigned rope. Kancha put me in the lead with the rope slung over my right shoulder, across my chest; its weight pressed down on my lungs and I struggled for breath. We marched off in the dim light over a knoll, to the base of the thousand-foot snow wall that led to the summit ridge of Island Peak. I was so cold I could not think beyond the next step. As I started to breathe hard in the thin air, I felt sick. Already, I was tired.

Sun began to touch some of the faraway peaks. In the dawn we could see the long, white wall waiting for us. The fixed rope snaked down from the snow onto the last pitch, which was rock, dangling in the air.

"We'll be taking turns here," explained Jim. "I'll go first. I'll climb that first pitch of rock and wait for you up on that ledge. Then you'll each climb past me. Good luck." He turned, in his bright yellow climbing suit, and made his way over the rocky debris to the wall. He clipped his jumar to the rope and started upward.

As I watched Jim creep up along the rock, I thought of Mt. Washington, half a world away, less than one-third the height of Island Peak. It seemed like ages ago that we had struggled against the wind, thinking we were getting ready for Nepal. New Hampshire seemed a hundred years away, somewhere in the distant past, along with all the people I used to know, in another world, another life. This was my world now: the climbing team, crampons, axes, backpacks, climbing strategy, the deep and unending cold. These were the only things that were real.

Jimmy, George, and Allen each boosted themselves up to grab the rope, and one by one crawled up the rock onto the ledge and into the snow. Then it was my turn. Sun had begun to inch its way down the long wall. I took that as a good sign. I glanced at Boyd and stepped over to the base of the wall. I grabbed the slick rope and clipped it to my jumar.

This is it, I thought. *Here we go.* I began the journey upward.

The rock was loose and my crampons alternately caught and slipped on the wall. (Although crampons are made for snow, we had to wear them to climb the rock on Island Peak because the snow slope above us would be too steep to stand on while putting them on.) Frustrated, I hurled my boot at the wall and sent showers of shale down into the gully below. I was working too hard, trying too hard. I told myself to relax. I breathed so hard I thought my head would explode. It seemed to take forever to get to the top of the rock; I felt as if I were under water. Damp air next to the rock chilled my lungs; dampness from the rock seeped through my gloves. Then I heard a shout and looked up the wall to my right. Jim was sitting on the ledge at the top of the rock wall. I turned and moved toward him. I reached the top, breathing so hard I was embarrassed, and turned away to hide it. I was desperate for water; my mouth was so dry that each breath sent needles up and down my throat. I took out my water bottle.

"Keep moving," ordered Jim. "You'll have to keep moving if you want to get to the top." I glared at him. His mood had changed. He was impatient, and I sensed that he would rather not have me on the mountain, slowing him down. But I knew we were making good time. I didn't say a word. I just kept drinking the water. Then I screwed the plastic cap back on my water bottle and stuffed it into my pack.

Altitude can make people testy, I remembered—*myself and Jim included.*

Anu appeared, smiling. "*Namaste,* Linda," he greeted me. His smile encouraged me.

"*Namaste,* Anu," I replied. I moved past Jim and clipped into the next pitch of rope, stepping into soft, deep snow. The slope was so steep that I could lean my knees against it. Steadily, I pushed up through the snow. Above me, I could now see Jimmy, Allen, and George working their way to the top. My lungs burned and my head pounded; but I did not let myself panic for air.

This is normal, I said to myself. *It will only last a few hours. Then I'll be at the top.* I was not dizzy or sick. *I'm fine,* I told myself.

Then Anu was above me, with his bright smile, his face against the ink-blue sky, saying something encouraging. I did not know what it was. I tried to smile back, then dropped my gaze to the snow. Breathe, breathe, step. Breathe, breathe, step. The soft shush-shush sound of the ice ax lulled me into a rhythm. I thought of the Sherpa saying about mountaineering: "Slowly, slowly is best." I let its rhythm carry me upward.

Then I didn't think anything at all for what seemed like a long time. George, Jimmy, and Allen were moving along the summit ridge now, tiny dots against the sky, the tops of their climbing helmets flashing in the sun. A thread of rope floated between them. Jim must have passed me, for he sat on the summit ridge, waiting for me. Suddenly, I had only a few feet to go. The snow was filled with tracks, ruffled by the climbers before me. I planted my ax for the last time, hoisted myself up, and swung around to sit on the two-foot–wide ridge. I strained to get oxygen into my lungs, breathing so hard I saw stars. But I was not sick. I knew I was all right. I rested and waited for Boyd.

He was crawling now, coming up the wall with Anu, as Anu's gentle musical voice eased him on. The altitude pressed heavily on him. A person's ability to adapt to altitude is inherited from parents; it is not determined by training. Being in good shape allowed Boyd to endure the pain, but it could not increase his body's ability to acclimatize. In agony, he drew himself up onto the ridge, shaking and gulping air. Tears eased down his cheeks. He had reached his personal goal: twenty thousand feet.

But he would not be crossing the ridge to the summit. He was dizzy, and it was simply too dangerous. The ridge was too narrow and the drop was a thousand feet. I recalled the decision we'd made to turn around on Mt. Washington. Now we had to make that decision again.

Without discussion, I unclipped from Boyd's rope and clipped my jumar to a rope with Jim and Kancha. Boyd clipped in with Anu for the return trip. I looked at Boyd, touched my mitten to his shoulder, and stood up. I started along the ridge.

I had never been on a rope with anyone but Boyd, and I was terrified that I would not recognize Jim and Kancha's signals and moves. I am also afraid of heights. I took my first steps onto the ridge, and as I did, I felt as though I were stepping into outer space. Like an astronaut tethered to a space ship, I walked slowly, weightlessly. The rope was heavy and blew around, tugging me off balance. I felt little or no connection to Jim and Kancha. I felt alone in outer space. I could not feel how fast I was going or how much ground we had covered. I could not bear to look off the ridge, so I looked at my feet, placing them carefully on the downside of the cornice (the overhang of snow at the top of the ridge). I began to think of my brother, who competes in triathlons. In a triathlon one summer, he swam through the Hudson River around the Statue of Liberty, rode his bike one hundred miles to Philadelphia, then ran ten miles to the Liberty Bell, in ninety-eight degree heat. I imagined my feet were his, pounding down the pavement in the shimmering

The snow wall and summit ridge leading to the top of Island Peak.

The summit, at last: Allen, Jimmy, Linda, and George. Kancha stands apart, saying prayers to the mountain gods.

heat, pushing to the end. When he finished the race, he didn't know where he was. Now I understood.

Concentrate, I said to myself. *Don't wander off this ridge.* I walked carefully, making sure not to step on the rope with my crampons, which could cut it. A small place inside me pushed me to the top. I thought I might be blown off the ridge like an insect, swept away into the deep blue sky. I forced my boots to move forward. I could not allow myself to stop. I could not allow panic. I was going to that little dome of snow, the summit. The ridge rose up a small knoll, and I thought I could not take one more step upward. Jim disappeared over the top and the rope tugged at my waist. In a dream, I followed. And then it was over. I was on the summit. Jim came back along the rope and threw his arm around my shoulder.

"Good job," he congratulated. Jimmy, Allen, and George came over to greet me.

"Where's Boyd?" asked Jimmy.

"He didn't make it—the altitude. He's on the ridge, taking pictures of us. Then he'll head back down to high camp with Anu." We hugged, shaking, through the bulky climbing clothes as carabiners caught and clanked against our waists and legs. Then I dropped my pack and unclipped from the rope, slipping my jumar into my pocket. I wandered around on the summit, ate a Rice Krispie bar, and peered over the edge at the tiny squares in the snow a thousand feet below: high camp. Wondering about Boyd's progress, I strained to see him on the wall. The great black Nuptse-Lhotse Wall towered five thousand feet above us and a whole galaxy of white peaks studded the horizon. The silence of the Himalaya sank into my soul. I took a long, deep breath. My heart finally quieted. I was on top.

We drew out our cameras and huddled in the brittle air while taking turns clicking off the shutters. Kancha stood apart, speaking to his gods. Then wind began to travel up the mountain, swirling around the top.

"We'd better get going," urged Jim. He tapped me on the shoulder. "Do you want to lead?" I nodded. We hoisted our packs, tromping around on the snow, carabiners jangling as we tightened our harnesses and gathered up the heavy ropes. I slung the weighty coil of rope over my shoulder.

We could not stay on the summit forever. We had to go down again. We had reached the summit of Island Peak: but our climb was only half over.

MOUNTAIN METHODS

Climbing Snow and Ice

Mountaineering sometimes involves climbing snow and ice. It may also involve technical climbing, which means climbing with a rope. Climbing snow and ice, whether technical or nontechnical, requires some special skills and equipment.

1. Walking up a trail in snow is different from walking up a dry trail. You have to lift your boots high. Sometimes you have to kick your boots into the slope, to create steps. Always wear waterproof boots to climb in the snow. You'll need stiff boots to hold crampons if the slope you're climbing becomes very steep or icy.

2. You need an ice ax when you climb in steep snow. An ice ax helps you balance and anchor yourself as you walk up and down steep slopes. It is also used for self-arrest (stopping yourself if you slip). Learn ice ax technique from an experienced climber before you attempt a steep mountain. For your first few climbs, rent an ice ax from a climbing-equipment store. After that, you'll have a better idea of what type of ax you want to buy.

3. Sometimes a mountain that you can climb without using a rope on one day requires a technical climb on another day because of bad weather, high winds, or icy conditions. If you have any doubt about the conditions and don't have a rope or don't know how to use one, then don't climb the mountain. A real hero is a person who knows when to turn around.

4. Climbing with a rope involves coordination between two or more people; this takes practice. The best way to learn technical climbing is through an instruction

program. There, you'll learn how to use a rope and harness, ascenders and descenders, crampons, and ice ax. Ask someone who works at an outdoor-equipment store if there are any courses given near you. Or write to one of the organizations listed in "Getting Started" at the end of this book. Finally, *never* try to use a rope other than a special climbing rope bought at a climbing-equipment store. Don't use clothesline or something else you have at home. Inadequate equipment could lead to serious injury.

16
Down the Mountain

I TOOK ONE last look around and stepped over to the edge of the ridge. I glanced back at Jim and Kancha to see if they were ready. Then I began the descent, taking tiny steps down the slope toward the knife-edge of the ridge.

I couldn't avoid looking down, and all the fear of falling came rushing back through me. Again I crept onto the low side of the cornice that arced off the ridge. (The high side would have been more dangerous, because it could break.) Suddenly, my whole body was weak and weary and I longed to be at the base of the mountain. I was losing my concentration. Alone at the head of the rope, I couldn't follow anyone else's track. I had to decide where we would all walk. I had to think. I became superstitious, not wanting to jinx the descent by becoming overconfident. We had been lucky to have such a smooth ascent, but I had to remember that the climb was only half over.

Each step was more careful than the one before as I inched along the snow, to Jim's impatience. "Commit yourself!" he shouted at me. I tried to take bolder steps, but with each movement I imagined myself pitching off the side of the ridge and hurtling toward the tiny tents at high camp below.

Somehow, I reached the point on the ridge where we had completed our ascent of the wall. The blue fixed-climbing rope lay in the snow, pinned to the wall by an anchor. I waited until Jim and Kancha joined me, then looped the rope around and through my descender (a metal tool used for climbing downward). I unclipped from the rope I shared with Jim and Kancha. I was ready to rappel down the wall. (Rappelling is a method of descending the rope in a controlled slide.) With my left hand above the descender and my right hand below it, near my waist as a brake, I turned to face the wall and leaned back with my legs perpendicular to the wall, my crampons digging in. I stepped off.

The rope slid quickly through my hands in little jerks. I stopped and started; stopped and started, leaning out and away from the wall, balancing myself with my feet, my crampons now touching the wall lightly. The rope grew hot in my hands, rubbing away the red fabric of my gloves. The movement became smoother, and soon I was sailing down, down, down the soft snow toward the base. Then I stopped short and looked over my shoulder. I had reached the end of the first pitch (rope length), about a hundred feet from the top of the wall.

I clipped into the second rope and unclipped from the first, making sure that my harness was always attached to a carabiner on one of the ropes so that if I slipped, I would not fall. Then I began to descend again, gliding down the rope, feeling jubilant and alive. I had done it. I had climbed the mountain. I had been to the top and seen the world from there. Now I was on my way down to Boyd and to safety. I knew he was watching, but I couldn't see him yet.

I bounced down the wall, reaching the end of the second pitch. I stopped and clipped to the third. Now I was into the rhythm of the descent, getting the hang of it, clipping and unclipping faster, without fumbling. I had never done such a long rappel with so many pitches. At the fifth pitch, Nima was there, ready to help. I waved him away and he laughed. He had been running up and down the snow wall ready to assist everyone, unroped, like a mountain goat.

I ticked the wall with the front points of my crampons to keep from swinging around on the rope. Slowly I eased the rope through my tattered red gloves. The wall that had taken so many hours and so much effort to climb slid by beneath my feet and hands so easily. Finally, I reached the end of the last snow pitch, right before the wall turned to rock. As I looked up from my task, Anu was there to greet me with a warm smile and help me make the switch to the rock. By now, I was happy to have help. His smile reassured me and I knew I was almost there. Above me, the others sailed down the wall at intervals.

I peered over the edge of the rock pitch and saw Boyd. I waved, but couldn't tell whether he could see me. Then I picked my way over the sharp rock and around to the final rope. I lifted it and clipped in for the final time, turning to face the rock wall. I leaned back and stepped off, sliding down through the nasty scree.

Suddenly my legs gave out; I swung like a giant pendulum in a clock, from side to side, twirling on the rope, kicking out at the wall to try to steady myself. Gradually I swung to a halt and hung there, feeling like a fool. I shuddered. I was more tired than I knew. It took a few minutes to regain my balance. My wrists ached from handling the rope and my calves were weak. My breath came in gasps. I shook with exhaustion and excitement. I was almost there.

I just want to get to the bottom of this, I thought. The summit seemed like a faraway dream.

I gripped the rope and began to descend again, hurling my boots at the rock, trying to bend and bang my crampons.

I never want to wear these things again, I thought bitterly.

In a final push, I swung out and down, hitting the ground with a thump. Shaking, I unclipped for the last time and wobbled over the shale to the snowbank where Boyd sat. I looked at the palms of my gloves: the cloth was ripped to shreds and the skin of my hands showed through, pink and blotchy. The rope had burned right through them. I stepped onto the hard snow and Boyd stood up with his arms wide open. I fell against him and he guided me over to a flat rock, helping me sit down.

I couldn't talk. I was numb. Boyd opened his water bottle and handed it to me. I couldn't remember when I'd last had a drink or something to eat. The strong sun eased into my aching muscles and I leaned against Boyd, gazing back up the wall where the others continued to descend, each like a spider clinging to his own web of rope.

Boyd and I had flown halfway around the world and walked two weeks for this day. We had climbed the wall together, yet there was now a distance between us. I had walked the ridge alone. I did not know whether or not he was disappointed about not reaching the summit. But I was sure that he did not regret his decision. It is one of the hardest decisions a mountaineer has to make. It is always easier to decide to keep going.

Gradually each member of the team swung out and dropped off the end of the last rope, landing in the scree with a dull thud. They walked over to the snowfield, their crampons ringing on the rock. Anu and Nima hurried on to high camp. Allen and George shook my hand. Jimmy hugged me tight and shook Boyd's hand. We were down. Jim joined us, and we packed up to head down the snowfield toward high camp. Jim let us go unroped, which bothered Allen.

"I think we should rope up here," Allen muttered. "The snow slope is steep and there might be crevasses." But he didn't say anything to Jim. Soon we reached high camp, where Anu and Nima were already cooking lunch. We threw ourselves on any surface and went to sleep. It was only 12:30, but already we'd had a full day.

"Lunch!" called Nima. I sat up in the sun, stiff and clumsy in my heavy clothes. I wasn't looking forward to the watery noodle soup, but I was hungry and needed nourishment. I sipped the soup slowly as it steamed into the crisp air. Then I cut the noodles with the edge of my spoon, shoveling them into my mouth methodically.

After lunch, we broke camp. We dragged our duffels out into the snow, wrenched the tent poles out of the ice, and the green nylon of the tents billowed out into the breeze. We patted the flapping tents down to the snow and rolled them tight, brushing away snow and ice. Soon nothing was left of high camp except the tracks of our crampons. We started down to base camp, still nearly five hours away. Tired, light-headed, and light-hearted, we stumbled toward the rock outcrop where we changed from plastic mountaineering boots to hiking boots. I stuffed the heavy boots into the bottom of my pack and laced up the familiar hiking boots. They felt like sneakers, they were so light compared to the mountaineering boots. I lashed my crampons, ice ax and heavy parka to the outside of my pack. Then I stood and began to pick my way down among the boulders, heading toward the steep slope that led to base camp.

George and Jimmy charged down the mountain and were soon out of sight. Somewhere in the distance, the deep, heavy rumble of an avalanche pounded through the silence. Later, we discovered that a chunk of the snow wall on Baruntse had split and fallen away in a giant slab avalanche, the worst and most dangerous kind. We had heard many avalanches in the Himalaya, but none had been so close. It reminded us that avalanches can happen anywhere there are snowy mountains and steep slopes, and any time the right temperature, snowstorms, and wind conditions combine. Although we couldn't know this now, a year after our trip a huge snowstorm would kick off an avalanche that would tumble all the way down the gully of Island Peak base camp, killing several climbers there. I wandered along the brown, barren slope with Jimmy and Boyd.

We've done it, we've done it, I said over and over to myself. The wind increased, pushing the fog up the long valley. Hours after we had begun, we trudged over the loose rock and down into base camp.

Relief spread through our team as we gathered for dinner. Pasang had done his best for us, and we ate enthusiastically, but without much conversation. There wasn't much we needed to say. We had gone up the mountain, and we had come down again. I thought back to Anu's comment as we crossed the Khumbu Glacier the week before: "This is success in a climb. When no lives are lost, that is success."

MOUNTAIN METHODS

About Avalanches and Crevasses

Everywhere there are snowy mountains and glaciers, there will be avalanches and crevasses. An avalanche is a mass of snow, dirt, and ice that breaks loose and rushes down a mountain. A crevasse is a deep crack or gap in the ice of a glacier.

Avalanches

There are two types of avalanches: loose snow and slab. The slab avalanche is the most dangerous because a whole section of snow slope breaks and slides. Most avalanches take place right after a heavy snowstorm. It may take several days for the snow to stabilize. Beware of *wet* snow slides after a rainstorm. If you are climbing in very high winds and very low temperatures, beware of windslab—crusty snow drifts—forming on slopes and ridges above you. Steep gullies and smooth, open slopes are the places avalanches are most likely to occur.

It is much better to avoid an avalanche than to try to survive one. If you must, cross suspicious slopes one person at a time, quickly. If an avalanche starts, don't try to outrun it. Hurry to the side of the slope. If you are caught, discard your equipment and let the avalanche come at you from behind. When it hits, try to stay in a sitting position, moving your hands as if you were treading water. If you are buried when the avalanche stops, take a deep breath and make a large air pocket in front of your face right away, before the snow settles. Then shoot one arm straight up to try to break through the surface. Don't yell—you'll use up your air. If you're not caught in the avalanche but someone else is, make a quick search by scuffling along the snow with your feet. Look for a hand or piece of clothing. Try to mark the spot where the person was last seen. Don't go for help unless you have a large group and can spare someone from the search. The person could be dead by the time help arrives. Think of *yourself* as the rescue team.

Crevasses

If you are climbing in an area where there are crevasses, you should be roped. The middle of a glacier usually has the fewest crevasses. If you see a crevasse, your party should cross at a right angle to the crevasse.

A winter climbing course should teach you about avalanche and crevasse rescue, including the use of rescue beacons.

17
Return to Pheriche

WE THOUGHT our adventure was over. We were wrong. True, climbing was behind us. But two days ahead lay Pangboche (Pang-bo-chay), the ancient monastery that claimed to possess the authentic scalp of Yeti (Yeh-tee), the legendary abominable snowman of the Himalaya. If we asked around and paid a few rupees, we heard, one of the monks might show us the scalp. We were determined to find it.

But that was too far off to think about. We slept late the morning after the climb, to Jim's frustration. He was right in his attitude that we had a long day's hike ahead of us and still another week's walk back to Lukla. But we didn't care. We rose after sunup and traipsed around camp, collecting trash left by the other party that had shared the base camp with us. Our hearts were light with the knowledge of our triumph, and we would have agreed to do just about anything. But I grew dizzy because of the altitude each time I bent over to pick up a wad of paper so I shuffled around, trying to avoid the chore. Within an hour, we had tossed old cans, used tea bags, and cellophane wrappers in a pile. Dendi touched a blazing stick to the whole mess and it ignited into a weak bonfire, smoke billowing up into the crystal-blue sky.

We broke camp for what seemed like the hundredth time and I heaved my now filthy blue pack onto my sore shoulders. I was tired of carrying this load every day. I was ready to head down toward home. And I was tired of walking.

Jettha rounded up the yaks with a high, thin whistle and loaded them down. They lumbered, sturdy and uncomplaining, out of camp. Jettha followed, grazing the lazy ones with the end of his stick, urging them on in the musical tones of the Sherpa language.

The Nuptse wall loomed fierce and demanding above us, while Baruntse, stripped of part of its snow wall, stood forlorn in the sun. Boyd decided to set up his tripod and stay at base camp for a while, taking photos of these two mountains as well as Island Peak.

Allen and I started out together, ambling down through the parched valley toward Chukhung for lunch. We planned to make it as far as Pheriche by dusk. Ahead lay the ribbon of trail through dust and rock. Behind lay the cold, clean world of ice. Allen and I chatted, our voices small under the wide sky of the Himalaya. Hours passed. Gradually the others cruised by us, barreling down the trail, shouting greetings over their shoulders. Pasang swept by, the pots and pans clanking in his basket as he jounced down the hill. Boyd caught up and joined us as we reached Chukhung.

Pasang had already laid out the orange tarp, which by now was the flag that guided us to our meal stops. We entered the dirt paddock of a tea house and flopped on the ground. Purba and Dawa hurried out from the hut, balancing bowls of hot tunafish, round slices of fried potatoes, and a jug of hot orange squash, setting them all on the ground. Little puffs of dust rose as he set the food on the tarp. Ignoring this, we dug in, but there didn't seem to be enough to satisfy our hunger. We polished off lunch in a few minutes. Then Jimmy flexed and curled like a cat, and sank quickly into a nap. George leaned back against the stone wall and read an old issue of *Climbing* magazine. Jim wandered across the yard to talk to some American college students who seemed to be trekking. Boyd, Allen, and I talked casually, lazing on the tarp.

Eventually, we glanced at our watches. We wanted to reach Pheriche in time for the daily altitude lecture at 3:30. It was already 1:00. We grabbed our packs and sped out to the trail. George and Jimmy were soon out of sight, their legs pumping hard down the path.

We came to an icy, blue-white brook, its water rolling over patches of snow and glistening rock. I hopped quickly from rock to rock, careful not to lose my balance. A fall in the river now, far from any camp or shelter, could mean hypothermia. Hypothermia means that the body's internal temperature has dropped way below normal. The most common way of getting hypothermia is by getting wet, because a chill sets in and the body cannot get warm. This can happen if a person is caught in a rainstorm, falls in a stream, or spends a long time sitting or lying in snow. Hypothermia can also set in if the person hasn't had enough food and water for the body to create energy for heat. Signs of mild hypothermia are cold hands or feet and uncontrollable shivering. Signs of more severe hypothermia include stumbling, poor coordination, a lack of caring about the situation, and trouble speaking or remembering. Severe hypothermia results in a low pulse and breathing rate; by that point, the person is very near death.

By the time we reached Dingboche, which lay on the other side of the hill from Pheriche, the silvery fog of afternoon was gliding up the valley, engulfing fields, stone walls, huts, and a slender *chorten* (a stone shrine honoring Buddha) that stood outside the settlement. For a moment, the clouds broke and a dazzling ray of sun splashed against the *chorten,* washing it in gold; then the clouds reunited and the *chorten* was gone. We clambered up the trail toward the top of the hill, zigzagging as quickly as we could, skirting rocks, passing to the left of *mani* walls. As we crested the hill, George and Jimmy plummeted down the other side, leaping down switchbacks, glissading down yak trails, their whoops and yells echoing up the valley. Boyd, Allen, and I followed, steaming back and forth along the trail, running, nearly tripping down the long, steep slope among the tangled scrub brush clinging to the loose dirt. Below us lay the Himalayan Rescue Association, its dull metal roof looking scruffy in the gray afternoon. Finally, we tumbled down the last bit of slope and jogged around to the front door, leaning on the pitted wooden door to open it. We squeezed into a crowded, hot room.

"So you should walk slowly, making sure to take a rest day for every thousand feet you climb," Ben was saying. He stopped and turned to see what the commotion was. Our eyes met and a grin broke across his face. I nodded and moved to the back of the room, pressed against the wall as he continued his lecture.

Crushed among the new trekkers, we felt like old hands. We'd already been here. We had climbed our mountain. Yet just a few weeks ago we had been on our way in, just like these people, not knowing what lay ahead. Their faces were eager and intent, taking in everything Ben said. Afterward, they raised their hands to ask questions. This might be the most important classroom of their lives.

"I've had a headache for two days," one trekker said. "What does that mean?"

"I'm not thirsty," said a young woman. "Does that mean I've been drinking enough water?"

"I feel dizzy when I stand up," said another. "I'm also out of breath all the time."

Ben answered their questions patiently. Eventually the group broke up and he was able to make his way over to us.

"Hi there," he said, and stuck out his hand to shake mine. "How did you do?"

"We made it." I grinned. He gently slapped my shoulder and shook everyone else's hands.

"Good going. Are you staying in Pheriche tonight?"

"Yes," answered Allen. "We're camping across the road."

"Then have dinner here with us," invited Ben. Bill and Judy appeared and greeted us all around. When the last trekker had left, Judy stocked the small wood stove with cedar and disappeared into the dark passageway leading to the kitchen. The spicy wood crackled and hissed inside the stove. We arranged ourselves on benches and stools close to the stove, soaking up the warmth. Soon Judy returned with a large pot of tea swinging from her hand and a tray of mugs, canned fish, and biscuits for appetizers. She set the tray on the floor near the stove and poured cups of tea, passing them around. With our penknives, we scooped the fish out of the can and positioned it on the biscuits, biting into the cold, oily flavor.

The door swung open and slammed the wall behind it. In walked Jim, followed by Pasang, who carried a tin pot filled with white, fluffy *makai*.

"Hi," he greeted Ben, Bill, and Judy. "Is there room for a table in here?" he asked, looking around.

"Sure," replied Bill, waving his arm. "Along the back wall." Pasang set the pot of *makai* on the floor and left. A few minutes later he was back with Purba, balancing the table we occasionally used for meals. They eased it through the doorway sideways, lifted it around the stove, and flipped open the legs, standing it near the wall. Dawa entered, carrying several folding stools. We got up and helped him place these around the table.

Pasang, Dawa, and Purba left, but returned an hour later carrying huge tin trays piled high with food. One pot contained nearly a hundred cheese *momos,* warm and chewy. Another bowl held thick, homemade french fries and cooked green beans. We passed around plates and heaped them full with food. We talked about climbing and rock & roll songs as we ate, filling ourselves until we could eat no more, then washing it all down with black tea.

Then Pasang brought in bowls of fruit cocktail. Ben turned on the old radio that hung in a corner against the wall. The BBC

(British Broadcasting Company) broadcast news every night at 8:00, from the other side of the world. Far off, countries fought each other, leaders were elected, business deals were made, storms swept across oceans and continents. The news sounded so unreal, so far away from this world where from day to day we worried only about finding the trail, staying healthy, and keeping warm and fed. We were happy to be where we were. Eventually, we straggled out into what had become a clear, crisp night. We marveled at the stars glittering in the deep black sky. Yes, we were much happier to be here.

The next morning, Jim sent word to meet him at the Snow Lion Hotel, where we would have breakfast. We ducked into the dark, cramped house, parted some grimy curtains, and stepped into a smoky, musty room that was the kitchen. A grubby, somber little boy with a runny nose and cough served us lukewarm milk tea in murky Flintstone glasses. A woman shuffled in with a tray of hard-boiled eggs, cold cereal, and a pot of hot cereal. Then she hunkered by the fire, poking at the embers with a stick. Her son stood by her side, wiping his nose with his hand. Pasang arrived, carrying a pot of pancakes. We slapped them on plates and bit into them; they were heavy and cold. We downed them quickly and escaped from the darkness into daylight.

"It's time for a shower," declared Jimmy. It had been weeks since we had been clean. A small tin stall sat right at the side of the road, bearing a sign that read "hot shower." Jimmy slipped into the tea house next to it and ordered showers all around, including one for Dendi.

"You pay?" asked Dendi, his eyes sparkling. Jimmy agreed. Dendi was delighted. He hadn't had a hot shower in a long time. A shower would cost him a day's wages because water in the Khumbu is so precious. It must be carried or pumped a long way uphill from the river, so it must be used sparingly, mostly for cooking and drinking. Also, water for bathing must be heated, which uses up fuel. So most showers are taken by tourists—trekkers and climbers such as us—instead of the Sherpas. Not wanting to abuse this special privilege, we limited ourselves to one or two showers each on the entire trip.

After about twenty minutes, the owner of the tea house and shower ran outside and across the road, climbed a teetering ladder, and dumped the water into a bucket that tipped over and rushed down a pipe into the shower. Jimmy stripped to his underwear and leapt into the tin stall. I was tempted. I imagined the warm water streaming over my skin and all the trail dirt collecting around my feet in a puddle. But I decided not to take a shower here. For this shower, you had to undress in the road. I decided to wait until we reached Namche Bazaar, where I could undress in the relative privacy of the backyard of the Khumbu Lodge.

Over the next two hours, the men emerged, gleaming and clean, flipping their towels at each other. The tea-house owner ran back and forth with a new basin of hot water for each shower. Finally, Dendi emerged with a wide smile and his hair dripping. We were ready to pack up and break camp.

We walked back to the Himalayan Rescue Association to say good-bye to the doctors.

"Promise me you'll write and tell me how you are," insisted Ben. "Here's the name of a doctor I want you to see at home. Find out what caused your allergic reaction."

I promised. Judy handed me a packet of letters to mail to family and friends once we got back to the United States. They feared that their mail would not make it past Kathmandu because the local postal workers often steam the stamps off and resell them. So we said good-bye to new friends whom we would probably never see again. We started down the trail, across the river and toward Pangboche, determined to find the mysterious Yeti scalp.

MOUNTAIN METHODS
Frostbite and Hypothermia

Frostbite and hypothermia are two conditions to watch for and prevent when you are climbing. Frostbite generally happens in winter, but hypothermia can occur any time of the year.

Frostbite

Frostbite sets in when your skin and tissue beneath the skin freeze. Your fingers, toes, nose, ears, cheeks, and chin are the most likely parts of your body to freeze.

Symptoms. Frostbite starts with a cold feeling in a specific area (such as fingers or toes) that then turns to numbness. You might see white patches on the skin. If frostbite is severe, the affected area becomes rock hard.

Prevention. Drink plenty of fluids and eat enough so that your body has energy to keep producing heat. Wear loose-fitting clothing, including socks. If it is windy, wear a scarf around your face and make sure your hat covers your ears.

Treatment. Rewarm the frostbitten area with a warm hand or mitten. If your fingers are frozen, slip them into you armpits; don't rub a frozen area. If frostbite is severe, wait until you can get medical help before rewarming.

Hypothermia

Hypothermia occurs when your body temperature falls below normal. If it drops too low, your heart, lungs, and brain will not be able to function. Wet clothes, exhaustion, and lack of food and water can cause hypothermia.

Symptoms. Cold hands and feet, and shivering are the first signs of hypothermia. Stumbling, poor coordination, and trouble speaking, remembering, and thinking are further signs. Low pulse and breathing rate are signs that death is near.

Prevention. Always carry rain gear. Change from wet clothes to dry ones. Wear a hat. Drink and eat enough. Know that drugs and alcohol will lower your body temperature.

Treatment. Find shelter from wind and rain. Get into a tent and sleeping bag if possible. Change into dry clothes. Drink warm liquids and eat a snack. If anyone in your party has severe hypothermia, get the person to a hospital as soon as possible.

18
Yeti:
The Abominable Snowman

I IMAGINED the abominable snowman to be huge, white, and furry, like a polar bear.

"No," declared Anu, gesturing with his hands, his prayer beads dangling from his fingers. "Long black hair. Walks like this." He imitated an ape.

Yeti must be like Bigfoot, I thought.

The Sherpas don't believe there is one single Yeti. In fact, they believe that there are three *kinds* of Yeti. The smallest type of Yeti is called *thelma* (tuh-hel-ma). This Yeti lives in the thick, dark forests below ten thousand feet elevation and travels in groups. It climbs trees and hoots wildly though the forest. It also looks very much like a monkey, and many people believe that it actually is a monkey. But to see a *thelma* is considered bad luck; and no one wants to take that chance.

The largest Yeti is called *dzu-teh* (chu-tay). *Dzu-teh* is reported to be nearly eight feet tall with shaggy fur that can be blonde, red, black, or gray. It can walk on its hind legs or drop to all fours, and wanders among the foothills of the Himalaya at altitudes above thirteen thousand feet. It has long, sharp claws and sometimes attacks yaks belonging to Sherpas. In Sherpa language, *dzu* means "cattle" and *teh* means "ape." So *dzu-teh* is the ape who preys on cattle (in Nepal, yaks).

Mih-teh is the Yeti that everyone thinks about. This Yeti stands tall on its hind legs, walking like an awkward person. Woolly black or red fur covers most of its body, except for the face. It wanders high among the Himalaya, between fifteen thousand and eighteen thousand feet, making a high-pitched wail that echoes up the valleys. In Sherpa language, *mih* means "man." So you could say that *mih-teh* means that this Yeti is the "ape who is like a man." Or you could say that *mih-teh* is the "ape who preys on man."

For many years, people have reported sighting the Yeti. Explorers have tried to track it down; scientists have tried to study it. In

1921, while searching for a route up Everest, George Leigh Mallory saw giant footprints in the snow. In 1951, the great British explorer Eric Shipton stumbled on fresh tracks embedded in a glacier. "Yeti," announced his Sherpa guide. Sherpa Sen Tensing then told about how he and several other Sherpas had seen a Yeti near Tengboche nearly two years before. Shipton took photos of the tracks but never saw the Yeti.

Climbers and explorers kept going to the Himalaya, kept hearing stories of the Yeti, and even saw tracks. So in the winter of 1960, Sir Edmund Hillary, along with climbers and scientists, went to the land he knew and loved so much to search for the Yeti. The Sherpas often said, "Look on a Yeti and die." But Hillary and his team were determined to set the record straight.

They set up camps from where they could observe the area and any Yeti that might come into view. One day, two Sherpas ran into a camp crying, "*Yeti sahib! Yeti sahib!*" (*Sahib*—pronounced "sahb"—means "sir.") The team gathered up cameras and measuring equipment and quickly followed the Sherpas to the spot where the tracks had been, but the tracks had melted.

Then one of the scientists found another set of tracks on a glacier. When he looked closely, he discovered that the part of the tracks that lay in the sun looked like those of a Yeti, but the tracks that lay in the shade looked like those of a fox.

Not long after this, a nun offered to let them see a Yeti fur that she claimed she owned, but they would have to pay a price. When they arrived to see the fur, the nun suddenly said she knew nothing about a fur. Several monks decided they could solve the problem. After haggling, the monks, the nun, and the scientists reached an agreement. The nun brought forth a thick black fur with a light stripe across its shoulder. The scientists fingered the fur and examined it carefully. It was the fur of a bear.

Hillary and his team heard that the monks at Khumjung treasured a Yeti scalp that they claimed was 240 years old. In nearby Pangboche, the monks had another Yeti scalp.

The team went to Khumjung. The scalp looked like a leather helmet with patches of coarse, sharp, dark red hair. The scientists were curious. Now they wanted real proof that the scalp belonged to a Yeti. They told the monks that they wanted scientists from around the world to examine the Yeti scalp. The monks were suspicious and didn't want to let the scalp go. They argued and bartered. Finally, Hillary's team and the monks struck a deal. Hillary's group could take the scalp, but it must be returned within six weeks—not a day later. Several of the expedition's Sherpas must put their homes and all other possessions under the supervision of the monks. If the scalp was not returned within the specified time, the Sherpas would give up everything they owned. It was also decided that Sherpa Kunjo Chumbi, a prominent citizen, must travel with the scalp on its journey around the world.

After agreeing to all this, Hillary, Kunjo, and several other members of the expedition raced down the valley to Kathmandu. (There was no airstrip at Lukla at the time, so they had to walk all the way.) They loaded the scalp on a plane and flew halfway around the world to Chicago. Later, they traveled to London and Paris to visit scientists there.

Kunjo had never been so far away from home. He marveled at all the new things he saw, heard, ate, and experienced. In Chicago, he saw his first television. In London, he was frightened by the loud roar of the subway. When he visited the British royal palace, he pointed to the palace guards and exclaimed how odd it was that they wore huge black hats made of Yeti scalps. In Paris, when he realized that the scientists did not believe the Yeti scalp was genuine, Kunjo said wisely, "In our villages people do not believe in giraffes and lions because there are none in Nepal. And so you don't believe in Yetis. We can appreciate your ignorance."

But all the scientists agreed that the Yeti scalp was a fake. It was probably molded from the skin of a goat. With this decision in hand, Hillary, Kunjo, and the others sped back to Kathmandu. Their deadline was January 5, 1961. They arrived in Kathmandu on December 31. They had only six days left and it normally takes nearly two weeks to walk to the Khumbu. Fortunately, two Americans offered to lend them a helicopter they had been using. But storms blew in, so for the next few days the group was stranded, biting their fingernails and tapping their feet. Finally, the morning of January 5 dawned clear. The helicopter lifted into the air and sailed smoothly among the peaks, racing up the Khumbu Valley toward Khumjung. Then in a whirl of dust it touched down, the propellers whopping and humming, and Hillary and Kunjo leapt to the ground with the scalp. Solemnly they presented it to the monks, within hours of the deadline. The Sherpas' homes had been saved.

The scientists' verdict didn't matter a bit as we hiked along the trail toward Pangboche. Anu strolled along with us, explaining local sights and objects as we went.

We came to a tall flagpole. On top of it was perched a white, blue, and orange cylinder with a long white prayer flag streaming down from it.

"A lama, or special monk, declared this a good place for a village," said Anu, "based on signs from Buddha. But there was no money to build a village. So the flag marks the place. If people come later and want to build a village, they will know that this is a good place to begin."

Down the trail we passed a group of crude stone pillars. "People are cremated here. Then sometimes the ashes are thrown into the river below." I peered down more than a thousand feet to the gushing Dudh Kosi. Its distant roar drifted up to where we stood. "Sometimes the ashes are made into ink for prayer flags," Anu went on. And so prayers are carried to Buddha by loved ones who have died.

A large, intricately carved *mani* stone was propped near the trail. Anu explained that if a person wishes to have a *mani* stone carved, he or she pays a stone-carver to do so. Anu has several *mani* stones scattered throughout the Khumbu. "If a ghost is fighting me in my future life and I am running from the ghost, I will run to my *mani* stone and the stone will stop the ghost and turn it away."

As we neared Pangboche, Anu pointed to a cluster of small stone houses hugging the hill far up to our right. "Holiday houses," he called them, waving his arm. Older men go to these houses to pray for a season or two. It is like a religious retreat. Ang Lamu's father did this for several seasons before he died.

I pushed up my sleeves. It was near midday and the sun was burning strong. We rounded a corner and there was Pangboche. Its squat, brick red buildings rested on terraces cut into the side of the hill like shelves, surrounded by bare, gnarled rhododendron trees. Pangboche is ancient, the oldest *gompa* or monastery in the Khumbu. It may even be one of the oldest in Nepal. Legend says that the lama came to Pangboche in the form of a crow and landed there, declaring it a good site for a monastery. We trotted through narrow pathways as we entered the village. Nima caught up with us and George, Jimmy, Jim, and Allen appeared from behind several trees where they had been waiting for us. Nima seemed to know what to do and told us to wait where we were. He disappeared among the winding streets so we dumped our packs and sat on them to wait. A few yards away, a small boy, his pants split and his diapers peeking through the rip, held tight to the string of a kite as the kite pitched and climbed in the breeze. Suddenly, the kite dashed to the ground and the boy ran to grab his mother's hand. She bent to rub the dirt from his face, and together they walked inside their home.

Nima returned and motioned us to follow him. We wound our way through narrow pathways and came to the *gompa*. An old woman, her face as worn and gnarled as the trees of Pangboche, met us at the door. She turned and we followed her past a clump of bedrolls piled in the corner of the front room, obviously meant for junior monks. Candles flickered, their pungent yak-butter aroma filling the room. Burning incense and dust wafted up toward the filmy windows. Portraits of the king and queen hung in the center of the room from beams the width of tree trunks, with prayer flags draped over them.

We climbed a worn, slippery ladder to an upper room. The walls were lined with hundreds of sacred books that were brought out, dusted, and read by the monks at special occasions. Wild, brightly painted masks hung on the walls; these would be used in celebrations such as Mani Rimdu at Tengboche. The whole room was painted in colorful scenes of Buddhist life.

Nima and Anu faced the life-sized Buddha that watched over the dimly lit room. They touched their foreheads, lifted their hands in prayer, then knelt with their foreheads touching the floor. Anu rose and slipped a ten-rupee–note offering into the space between the Buddha's feet. Nima inserted an offering into the wooden box that sat on a pedestal nearby. We copied him. The old woman stood by the box, tapping the slot in the top with each donation to make sure that the money dropped all the way in. Then she hobbled to a murky corner of the room and lifted the creaky lid of a trunk. She returned and set two objects on a table. We crowded around as she separated the objects and stood back. A cone-shaped object the size of a human head with straggly, reddish hair clinging to it and three round holes pierced through the top sat bathed in dim light. Next to it lay a child-sized, honey-colored claw. Boyd quietly positioned his camera at his waist and clicked the shutter. The woman's head swung around and her round, beady eyes glared at him. He put the camera away. I reached out and

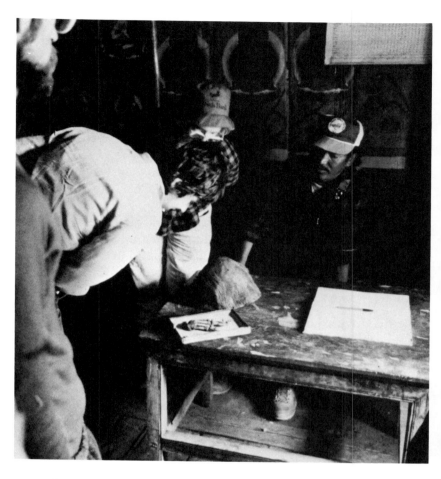

The Yeti scalp: a fake or the real thing?

fingered a patch of hair on the scalp. It was thin and wiry. Then the woman grabbed away her prize and hastily stashed it back in its locked box. We looked at each other, not knowing what more to expect. When nothing happened, we climbed down the ladder and filed back out into daylight, blinking.

"Didn't look like a goat to me," observed Jimmy.

"Didn't look like a monkey either," declared Allen.

"There's no proof that it's real," said George.

True enough. On the other hand, no one can prove that the Yeti *doesn't* exist. We shivered in the bright sun.

MOUNTAIN METHODS

When Things Get Too Hot: Heatstroke and Heat Exhaustion

When you hike in hot weather, you need to take measures to help keep your body cool. If your body overheats, you might get heat exhaustion or heatstroke. The best way to prevent both of these is to walk slowly, stop for rest, drink plenty of water, and eat salty snacks.

Heat Exhaustion

Heat exhaustion is your body's reaction to overheating, which includes salt-deficiency and dehydration (lack of enough water).

Symptoms. Symptoms include rapid heartbeat, nausea and vomiting, headache, dizziness or light-headedness, and pale, cold, or clammy skin. The body's temperature is not much above normal, if at all.

Treatment. Stop hiking and rest in the shade. Drink lots of water and eat something salty.

Heatstroke

Heatstroke is much more serious than heat exhaustion because the body's temperature has risen way above normal and its normal cooling system—sweat glands—is no longer working. Heatstroke is also called sunstroke.

Symptoms. Heatstroke may appear quickly, without warning. Symptoms include a pounding pulse, confusion, and hot, red, dry skin. Severe heatstroke can cause a coma leading to death.

Treatment. Heatstroke is a real medical emergency, but one that can be treated by hiking partners. If possible, soak the person in a cool but not cold stream or pond. Otherwise, soak bandanas and other cloths and cover the person with as many of them as possible. Massage the arms and legs to promote circulation that will help cool the vital organs such as the heart. All of these actions are designed to reduce the person's temperature. The person should rest after recovering and see a doctor as soon as possible.

19
Wash Day

PASANG SWITCHED ON his radio and we lounged on the orange tarp, eating lunch as the twangy strains of Nepalese and Indian music whined across the yard behind the Pangboche *gompa.*

Children peered over the stone wall and called *"Namaste!"*

"Namaste!" we shouted back, and they ducked behind the wall. Soon it was time to move on. We folded the stiff tarp, picked up our packs, and set out for Phortse (Fort-say), a tiny village where we planned to spend the night and the following day. Not many trekkers visit Phortse because it lies across the river from Tengboche and is thus a bit off the main trekking path. Phortse is famous in the Khumbu for its buckwheat crop (the only one in the area), just as Dingboche is known for its wheat crop. There is also a Hillary school in Phortse. Phortse has no electricity, but a long, black water pipe draws water a thousand feet up from the gushing Dudh Kosi below.

Protected by the deep shade of the dense forest the trail wound among the rhododendron trees. After weeks of barren earth, wind, ice, and snow, the woolly green of evergreens seemed even greener and softer than it had on the way in. The trail hugged the steep hill and we tromped up and down, under rock overhangs, in and out of the forest. Suddenly, we came to a traffic jam. Ahead, two yak trains had met on the same narrow path. One was headed up the trail and the other was headed down. (Jettha was way ahead with our yaks.) The yaks grunted and swayed, annoyed at being stopped. The yak drivers shouted and gestured. The trail was not wide enough for the two trains to pass each other. I had heard that in Nepal, if two yak trains met going the opposite direction and could not pass because the trail was too narrow, one had to be pushed off the path. In this case, it would mean a fall of more than a thousand feet. We waited expectantly. Then one of the yak drivers shoved his yaks tight underneath a rock overhang, leaning against them, jamming them against the wall. The other drove his yaks past, and they picked their way down the steep, rocky path.

On the other side of the river gorge lay Tengboche, peaceful in the gathering afternoon fog that was now rolling up the valley. As we dropped in elevation, the vegetation grew more lush, but the air was still dry and the trail rocky and dusty. Soon, Phortse appeared like a dream through the mist that was now so thick it was nearly a drizzle. Stone houses, stone roofs, stone fences, all in colors in muted brown and gray, lay behind a veil of mist. A few villagers drifted back and forth across the dirt pathways, their long tunics brushing the ground. Children's voices echoed across the dirt pastures as they burst from school at the end of the day. Anu walked behind us praying.

Following the outermost stone wall, we skirted the village and headed downward toward the river on a long switchback. Jim, Jimmy, Allen, and George had long since passed us, so Anu, Nima, Boyd, and I walked together. Many *mani* walls lay scattered here and there, piled high with *mani* stones offering prayers to Buddha. One was so large that Boyd and I didn't realize it was a *mani* wall and we walked around the wrong side. Anu and Nima disappeared and reappeared on the other side. Sheepishly, I giggled.

"We went the wrong way!" I exclaimed to Anu, shrugging my shoulders. They chuckled. Although we knew it was customary to walk to the left of the *mani* walls, the Sherpas never tried to press their religious beliefs on us, and because of that we tried hard to follow their customs, out of respect. And we felt all the more guilty when we failed.

Anu stopped short and pointed to a large bird that had fluttered into the forest, landing on the branch of a rhododendron. Its body was a dark, glossy blue-green with a bright tail of yellow feathers fanning out behind.

We walked deeper and deeper into the forest, where huge, haunting rhododendron trees, dripping with moss, bent over each other and the trail. Anu pointed to rich mushrooms bulging from the ground and told us how people eat them. Ahead, the clouds parted for a moment and the sky was aflame with color, the great peak of Cho Oyu (Choy O-Yoo) bathed in gold. Close by, the peak of Khumbila lay in shadow.

The clouds closed over the mountains again and we descended deeper into the mist. Suddenly an enormous Tibetan yak appeared out of the gloom. It stood staring at us, black and white, like a blend of earth and fog, with one horn twisted upward and one horn twisted down. This was a true yak—not the small, yak-cow crossbreed that we used for pack animals.

Eventually the trail opened into a flat clearing near a stream that led down to the river, although we were still a hundred feet or so above the real Dudh Kosi. Pasang, Dendi, and the others had set up camp, but it was deserted. We seemed to be the first to arrive although Jim, Jimmy, Allen, and George had long since passed us. I strolled around camp at dusk. It seemed like a paradise, isolated on a bed of evergreen needles.

The others arrived long after dark. They had stopped at a local tea house in Phortse. We squeezed into the meal tent and snacked on a pot of *makai* before dinner. Tomorrow would be our last day to rest, wash clothes, and repack our gear before the final push to Namche Bazaar and then Lukla. I lay in my sleeping bag that night, listening to the gentle rush of the river and the breeze brushing through the trees all around.

For breakfast the next morning, we hauled out the old table and set it on wobbly legs. Bundled in pile jacket and wool cap, I pulled up a stool and claimed a spot at the grubby tablecloth, whose contents now told the story of our entire trip. We passed around the bowl of hard-boiled eggs. I poured a stream of salt onto my plate and dipped the end of the cold egg into the little white pile. I flopped a few pancakes on my plate and spread honey on them, washing the whole meal down with tea. One of Jettha's yaks wandered over to the table, sniffling at the ground. It raised its head, nodding it back and forth. Jimmy turned to face it.

"Want an egg?" he asked the yak. He held out an egg toward the yak, which blinked at him. Then he dropped it on the ground and the yak rolled it around with its muzzle. Eventually, the animal decided it wasn't interested and wandered over to the bushes to join the rest of the herd. Pasang and Purba collected the pots that had held our breakfast and carried them over to the yaks, placing them on the ground in front of the animals. One of the yaks stuck its nose in the pot and lapped the pot clean in one swipe with its huge pink tongue. Then the yak lifted its head and plodded away. I wondered if this was how all our dishes had been cleaned during the trip. It didn't matter now.

After breakfast, we returned to the jumble of gear in our tents and dragged it all out, unzipped our sleeping bags, and draped them over the tents in the weak morning light. I collected a few stale clothes and decided to make a stab at washing them. These were the trekking clothes—cotton pants, polypropylene shirts, heavy socks—that I planned to give to the staff at the end of the trip, as is the custom on most expeditions in Nepal. I walked down the steep trail to the river, stepped out onto a flat rock, and squatted, dunking my cotton hiking pants in the frigid water, swirling them around. I pulled them out, slapped them on a rock, and did the same with the other clothes. I carried the wet heap back up the trail and hung each piece of clothing on a tree branch to dry in the sun.

Midmorning, Pasang offered me some of his homemade yak-butter tea. I sipped the sour, oily, salty liquid. When he wasn't looking, I tossed the contents of my cup into a bush.

As I sat on a cushion of evergreen needles near the tent, waiting for the clothes to dry, my mind drifted toward home. I thought of the comforts and possessions that now seemed foreign. I wanted to walk around without a package of Kleenex and butane lighter always stuffed in my back pocket. I longed for a sweet bubble bath, a haircut, homemade apple pie. I imagined riding in the car on a smooth, wide highway. I wanted to watch the news on television. And I wondered if all our friends and family had forgotten us; surely they had. It seemed as if we had been gone for a lifetime.

Below me, Dawa spent an hour at the cold, murky river. He washed and pounded his clothes in the water and stretched them carefully on the rocks to dry. He pushed his pants up to his knees and rolled up his sleeves to wash himself, dousing his head in the water, soaping up, rinsing, and shaking himself off like a dog.

I looked at the backs of my hands, which had become lined and cracked. My lips were now always chapped and dry. I decided to do a little work on my feet. I unlaced my boots, pulled them off, and rolled down my socks. The skin of my feet was pale and smudged; a ring of dirt circled each ankle. I peeled off the tape I kept on my heels to prevent blisters. I had been lucky this trip. I'd barely even had a "hot spot" or "soft spot" leading to a blister in three straight weeks of walking up and down steep trails. But my boots were light-weight, Gore-tex hiking boots that fit perfectly. I kept the tape on my heels with the backup of moleskin (padded tape) in my first-aid kit. I knew that if my heels and toes developed blisters, I'd have a hard time walking. Besides, the blisters could easily become infected in an environment where it was so hard to get anything clean. I had taken care of my feet and it had paid off. I sat back and wriggled my toes in the fresh air. A small dash of color caught my eye. A pink and yellow butterfly, soft as velvet, fluttered down to my sleeve. I watched it in wonder: so little wildlife could survive in this harsh country that a delicate butterfly seemed to belong in a different world. But Nepal is filled with its mysteries—and surprises.

MOUNTAIN METHODS

Blisters

As a hiker, you depend on your feet to carry you wherever you want to go. Walking with blisters on your feet is painful and difficult. When walking uphill, you may get blisters on your heel and the tendon at the top of your ankle. When walking downhill, you may get blisters on the tops of your toes.

Preventing Blisters

The best way to deal with blisters is to prevent them. Make sure that your hiking boots fit properly. If your boots are new, break them in slowly by taking short walks, especially if the boots are made of leather. Before starting out on a hike or climb, put a strip of wide first-aid tape across your heels; this will reduce the chances of developing blisters. Wear two pairs of socks: a light-weight, thin pair under a thicker pair.

Treating Blisters

If you develop a blister, stop to treat it. Otherwise, it will only get worse as you walk. Take out your first-aid kit. With your pocketknife, cut a hole the size of your blister in a piece of moleskin (padded tape). Peel the backing off the moleskin and place the moleskin on your foot with the hole over the blister. This will protect the skin but let the blister "breathe" If the blister has broken, clean it with soap and water. Then squeeze a bit of antiseptic clean cream on a piece of sterile gauze and tape the gauze over the area with the blister. Finally, cover the gauze with a piece of moleskin with the hole centered over the blister. When you reach camp or home, completely clean your foot and the blister to prevent infection.

20
Jim:
A Mountain Guide's Story

LATER THAT AFTERNOON, Jim told me the story of how he started to hike and later became a mountain guide. Jim had been hiking and camping since the seventh grade.

"When I was in elementary school, and even in the first year of junior high, I was very unathletic," Jim said. "I really liked reading, and I was pretty good in school. But I would get bullied, and I never went out for a sports team. In gym class, if it was baseball season, I was undoubtedly the last or second to last to be picked for the team."

In seventh grade, Jim got a job as assistant to the school librarian, which he loved because he could read all the new books first when they came to the library. One day, a book called *The Complete Walker,* by Colin Fletcher, arrived. Jim took it home to read. The book introduced him to backpacks, stoves, sleeping bags, and tents; and it explained why hiking and camping are so much fun. Jim read the book cover to cover, becoming more and more interested. Then for Christmas, Jim's parents gave him a backpack, sleeping bag, and stove, and he started sleeping out on the back porch in winter. Later that winter, Jim and a friend set off to climb Mt. Washington in northern New Hampshire. As they climbed, snow began to fall, soaking their blue jeans. (As he did more winter hiking, Jim learned to wear wool pants instead.) Then Jim organized a trip with three of his friends to Mt. Carrigain, also in northern New Hampshire. This time, they slept at the top, in the fire tower. Since Jim wasn't old enough to drive, he asked along a friend who could drive on these trips.

When he got to high school, Jim began to test his outdoor abilities further. He backpacked all through the White Mountains of New Hampshire, using the *White Mountain Guide* to show him the way.

"I started getting competitive with myself," he told me. "The guidebook listed the average time for each hike, and I would try to beat the time by a certain amount. Pretty soon I could cut the time in half, even carrying a full pack." He learned how to stay warm and dry in bad weather, and he found he even enjoyed living outdoors in tough conditions.

Jim and his friends began to wear hiking boots to school. "I was never really totally alienated, but this was one of the things I probably used to make friends with other kids. I emerged as a minor leader of the pack, in terms of backpacking," he remembered. "I read a lot about it and I would usually plan the routes for our trips. I also started to keep track of the four-thousand footers (mountains higher than four thousand feet) I climbed. The Appalachian Mountain Club has a special club for people who climb all of them, and that's great for a teenager, I think."

During the summer, Jim sold newspapers on the streets of Boston five days a week and then went to the mountains on weekends. "It was the only sport I could relate to, and it gave me a great feeling of confidence," he told me. "I knew I could go up there with people who were basketball players and probably hike faster and farther and carry more weight than some of them."

When Jim graduated from high school, he didn't know what to do. He thought he wanted to be a photographer, but he didn't think he was good enough to become a professional. He didn't know whether or not he wanted to go to college. He got a job in a factory and at the same time volunteered at a community mental-health center, where he worked on a hotline. Then he heard about a small, local group that was running a summer outdoor program for young people. He went to a meeting and was hired to assist the director of the program. He chose the routes for the hikes and led students up all the four-thousand footers in the White Mountains that he hadn't yet climbed. But at the end of the summer, college loomed ahead, so he entered reluctantly, without a clear idea of what he wanted to do with his life.

Jim was unhappy at college. "I just hated it. It hated *me*. I was failing courses. I'd always been intelligent, but now I realized I was totally undisciplined."

Right before the spring of his freshman year, Jim heard about the National Outdoor Leadership School (NOLS) in Wyoming. Here was something that sparked his interest. So Jim went to NOLS instead of returning to college.

Because he had been hiking and camping for five years, Jim went to NOLS thinking that he already knew a lot. "But it took me until the end of the trip to realize that I didn't really know any more than anyone else," he told me. The group camped and backpacked for thirty-two days in the Wind River range in Wyoming. Then they tried to climb the Grand Teton in winter conditions, where their instructor survived an avalanche. At the end of the course, however, Jim was recommended for the NOLS instructors course, which he had to take to become a NOLS or Outward Bound instructor.

Jim worked for Outward Bound and NOLS, as well as other programs, on and off for several years. Then he became interested in the highest mountains in the world: the Himalaya. Eventually, he took the money he had saved while working and set off on a seven-month trip through Asia on his own. Jim was twenty-four years old, and this was his first trip overseas. He spent three and a half months in Nepal and then went to Bangladesh and India.

When Jim got to Nepal, he wanted to see Mt. Everest, so he trekked to the Khumbu, hiked up Kala Pattar, crossed the Kongma-La, and climbed Island Peak. Then he walked along a remote trail to the southeast and flew back to Kathmandu. He spent a month in Kathmandu, made some friends there, and went on to India.

Jim didn't forget about Nepal. He flew home and worked for Outward Bound for the next two summers. But he was also beginning to realize that teaching outdoor skills and guiding was uncertain work. He never knew whether he would have a job the following summer, and during the rest of the year he had to scramble to find jobs at ski resorts and outdoor shops.

"Winter or summer, none of these jobs would pay very much," he explained. "They also require you to have an extreme life-style. It was difficult for me to maintain friendships because I would be away so much." He also discovered that most people who worked at these jobs were college students, who only needed summer employment. By this time, Jim had left college for good and needed to work year-round. For six or seven years, he had strung together a series of outdoor jobs. "At any moment you never knew what was going to happen next. The pay was generally very, very low, which didn't bother me at the time. I never owned a car, but I was generally happy most of the time. And I knew for sure that there was nothing I enjoyed doing more."

Then Jim met a woman who had just started her own adventure-travel company. She asked him to return to Nepal to see if he could design a program that would guide people on treks and climbs in the Himalaya. Jim went and is now the director of Himalayan programs for the company. "The reason I was drawn to working over here at first was that the trekking season in Nepal starts in October and goes through May. I structured our program so that I would have a job year-round. For people who try to freelance, it's still a tremendously rewarding thing to do for a while. It doesn't pay very well unless you make a lot of sacrifices. Then it can be an actual career."

Jim's advice to young people who are interested in guiding is: "Probably the best way to do it would be to try to establish a home base, such as Outward Bound or NOLS, and become associated with that one place. I do know people who are now in the administration of Outward Bound who don't have any exposure outside of Outward Bound, and that's too bad. But it's better in terms of getting a steady salary. Outdoor education in America doesn't pay well, but if you can live with that, it's not a bad way to go." According to Jim, some schools employ academic teachers who can also teach outdoor education part-time. Also, local youth centers often have outdoor programs for young people, and they may need staff. Finally, organizations such as the Appalachian Mountain Club, Sierra Club, Boy Scouts, and Girl Scouts rely on trained and qualified volunteers to lead trips and teach outdoor skills.

MOUNTAIN METHODS

So You Want to Be a Mountain Guide

You've read the story of Jim's life as a mountain guide, and you know how he got started in his career. To be a mountain guide, you must have thorough knowledge and experience in camping and mountain climbing, because the people you guide will be depending on you. To increase your knowledge, take an instruction course. One might be offered through your school, local YMCA or YWCA, or Outward Bound. Later, you can take a leadership-instruction course, such as one given by NOLS or the Appalachian Mountain Club. For more information on this, see "Getting Started" at the end of this book.

Now you know how to get started on becoming a mountain guide. But what does a mountain guide *do*?

1. A mountain guide leads a group of people on a safe, well-planned trip through the mountains.

2. The guide takes the responsibility for planning the trip: determining the route (based on the abilities of the people in the group), planning meals, checking weather reports and conditions in the mountains, and finding out as much about the area as possible (including special hazards such as bears or avalanches). If you think you are interested in this, ask some of your hiking friends to let you take over the planning of a group trip.

3. The guide knows safety precautions and basic first aid, especially for injuries such as blisters, hypothermia, frostbite, dehydration, heatstroke, and heat exhaustion. The guide also carries a first-aid kit with extra supplies for the group.

4. When making decisions, the guide always keeps in mind the safety of the group as a whole. The guide

may have to decide that the group must turn back without reaching the top of a mountain.

5. The guide never leaves the group to climb the mountain on his or her own.

6. In a technical climb, the guide usually climbs first to fix the ropes for others.

21
Yak Hats and Cinnamon Rolls

WE LEFT PHORTSE the next morning, headed closer and closer to civilization, passing more trekkers and villagers on the trail. On a hill above Namche, we came to the nearly deserted Everest View Hotel, a modern building nestled among the trees, with wide, clear windows offering a view of the great mountains. Some foreign businesspeople had built it, thinking they would attract the richest travelers in the world. All the building materials had to be carried in by yaks and porters. Once it was built, electricity was sparse. Worse yet, it took seventy porters five trips a day, a thousand feet down to the river and back, to supply water for the hotel. The owners of the hotel thought they would fly their guests in to save the guests the trouble and hardship of trekking. But when the guests arrived, they had to be given oxygen and put to bed immediately—they had altitude sickness because they had not acclimatized. So the richest travelers in the world did not flock to the hotel, and now it is open to the few trekkers who want a bed to sleep in. But most prefer to stay in tents or with the Sherpas in tea houses. After all, that is why they have come to the Himalaya.

Curious to see its inside, we wandered through. The chairs were bleak and dusty, the carpet dull and threadbare. No one was around, so we brushed the crumbs off a tablecloth in what looked like the restaurant and sat down. A man soon appeared with menus, which were scribbled in pencil on stiff, gray paper. The prices were high. We ordered corn soup, a couple of Cokes, and some tea. About twenty minutes later the waiter returned, clattering the little blue tea cups as he ferried them to us, setting them down on the table as gently as he could. The soup was pale and watery, with lone bits of corn resting on the bottom. I sipped it suspiciously. It had no flavor, although it was served in a beautiful Japanese bowl.

"The soup is watery, without much corn," Jim remarked to the waiter, before he could escape.

The waiter shrugged and answered in Nepali, "I am not the cook." He left.

The tablecloths must have been intended to be white but they were gray and greasy, like the waiter's shirt. He seemed to be a local recruit and probably would have been happier to work at a tea house with his friends.

I gingerly sipped the soup but could not get much down. The place was chilly and depressing. I couldn't imagine the days when all the porters trooped back and forth carrying the water from the river. Impatient to leave, I took my pack, paid our bill, and walked out into the sunshine and breeze. Boyd followed me and we hurtled down the hill to Namche Bazaar, where we felt as though we were slapped in the face by civilization. Trekkers, climbers, and villagers mingled in the streets outside open, bustling shops and lodges. We had been in the wilderness for so long that Namche seemed like a big city.

We wound our way down the steep path directly behind the rows of houses built on terraces. At a turn, a woman came out from behind a house and approached us.

"With Jim?" she asked.

"Yes," we answered. "Are you Lhakpa Dolma?"

She nodded and turned, intending for us to follow her. She was a friend of Jim's—her husband, a Sherpa guide, had worked with Jim on several trips—and she had arranged with Jim to cook lunch for all of us. We entered her house through a small door covered by a rug and climbed the soft, worn wooden ladder to the second floor. We stopped at a large tin basin of water, dunked our hands, and soaped them. Then we took turns ladling the cold, clean water over our soapy hands, shaking them dry. As we stepped into the main room, Jim, Jimmy, George, and Allen arrived.

I admired the huge, shining Chinese copper pots that held water for the family. On the far side of the room, on the highest shelf, lay a whole row of shiny pressure cookers given to Lhaka Dolma's husband at the end of each expedition for which he worked as a guide. Above the door leading to a smaller sleeping room in back there was pinned a fading black and white photo of Lhakpa Dolma's husband standing on the summit of Dhaulagiri (Dahl-a-geer-ee). He had since given up climbing and now served as a sirdar on treks. In the generation before his, he would have counted his wealth and social status by how many yaks he owned; now he counted it by how many sleeping bags and pressure cookers had been given to him by various expeditions. He stored the sleeping bags in cupboards made of wood and glass lining the back wall of the main room. Four goat carcasses hung from the ceiling, drying. The walls and ceilings of the house were neatly and tightly insulated with thatch, a kind of woven grass.

Lhakpa Dolma hurried over with trays of delicious food: a pile of rice; a pot of yak liver soup with potatoes, peas, and curry; heaps of freshly cooked spinach; and tomatoes and pickles arranged neatly on a tray. We spooned out the food and wolfed it down, seated on benches covered with soft Tibetan rugs around a low table. It was the best lunch we'd eaten in weeks. We didn't talk much as we savored the flavors of fresh—and different—food.

After lunch, a commotion sounded on the staircase and Lhakpa Dhiki, Ngorup's mother, rushed in to greet Jim. Lhakpa Dolma joined in the celebration, bringing us glasses and a pot from which she poured a hot white liquid into each glass. This was *chang,* the traditional country drink. I sipped the smooth, nutty liquid and lowered the glass; immediately, Lhakpa Dolma refilled it. We discovered that we could not even drink half a glass without a refill. Jim finally turned and tossed the contents of his glass out the window to the street. Lhakpa Dolma filled his glass again, giggling; again, he emptied it outside. To Jim and Lhakpa Dolma, this was a game. Her duty as a hostess was to keep his glass filled; how he emptied it was up to him. Then she left and returned with a small, hot canister filled with coals from the hearth fire and placed it in front of us. It was clear that we were going to be here all afternoon. From a sack she produced apples sent to her from her mother in the Solu region, south of the Khumbu, as well as a plate of yak cheese from Tibet, which tasted like salted twigs.

Finally, we got down to business. Once more, Lhakpa Dolma brought a sack to the table. In addition to having lunch, we were there to buy caps made of yak wool—for Lhakpa Dolma was a well-known knitter of hats. We fingered the coarse wool caps, the color of Nepalese tea, and made our choices. Then Lhakpa Dolma presented a hat to Jim as a gift.

Fog crept into Namche as we rubbed our hands briskly near the hot canister. Eventually, we thanked Lhakpa Dolma and felt our way to Anu's house for a dinner of noodle soup with bits of boiled yak meat floating in it, which none of us could eat. I barely forced down a few mouthfuls, not wanting to offend either Anu or his kind wife, Ang Lamu. (We didn't know whether she or Pasang had cooked the meal.)

After dinner, Boyd and I stayed to talk with Anu and Ang Lamu while the others went off somewhere in town to a birthday party for an Australian trek leader. I was feeling grimy, tired of noodles, and not in the mood for a party. Anu lit a smoky incense stick. Quickly the room filled with a heavy, sweet smell. Then he showed us books about several of the expeditions for which he had worked. One year, the wealthy leader of a Swiss expedition invited Anu to visit him in Switzerland. Anu went, climbing many mountains in the Swiss Alps.

"Did you like the Alps?" I asked.

Anu nodded. "Very nice," he answered. "But not very high." His gold tooth flashed as he chuckled.

I noticed a large drum hanging from a beam in the center of the room and asked Anu what it was used for. He and Ang Lamu explained that it was used during a special ceremony when a group of local monks stayed at their home for several days to read a special Buddhist text that would purify and bless the dwelling. Because Anu and Ang Lamu were required to feed and house the monks, this was an expensive undertaking, but to have the home blessed by the monks in this manner was a status symbol.

We chatted on in broken English and Nepali. Anu glanced at Ang Lamu and said to us, "We have friends in California. They trekked with us several years ago." He brought forth a couple of pictures. "I have sent them letters, by the letter writer in Kathmandu, but they have not answered. Ang Lamu is very much afraid they have died."

"Oh Anu, I'm certain they haven't died," I assured him. "I'll bet they have moved and haven't received your letters. Give me their address and I'll try to contact them." I copied the address in my notebook. Anu and Ang Lamu seemed relieved.

The others returned long after the town lights had shut off, and candles and incense burned dimly in the room. We had all decided to sleep here in the house instead of in tents. As I lay down on the wooden platform, pulling the coarse blanket up to my chin, I gazed outside. The sky was cluttered with stars. I fell asleep next to the glowing incense stick and a large box of eggs.

The next day, I was determined to have a shower. The best shower, we had heard, was at the Khumbu Lodge. So after breakfast I crossed the street and climbed the dark stairs to the third floor and stuck my head through the kitchen door, next to a large piece of raw meat.

"Shower?" I asked.

A young girl patted the hot-water pot and said, "Fifteen minutes."

So I went to the main room and ordered a cinnamon roll and tea while I waited for the shower water to boil. The cinnamon roll was large and sticky, with a hard crust of dark glaze on top, a soft and chewy inside, and hard chunks of cinnamon rolled between layers. As I tore open the roll, a sweet, spicy smell drifted upward.

After about a half hour, the girl called "Shower OK!" I raced down the three flights of stairs and out into the backyard, knowing that the water was following me down a pipe that led to the shower. I stopped short. In the yard, which was piled high with firewood and drying yak dung, another girl was cleaning out the small wooden cubicle with the sign "hot shower" nailed to its side. She brushed the floors and walls hard, then left the brush on the floor of the shower stall. She bailed out the ankle-deep, leftover water with a large tin pan. Then she stepped back.

"OK, now," she said, motioning to me. I tugged off my clothes and hopped into the damp, chilly stall. After a frantic, two-minute shower, the water slowed to a trickle and then died. I toweled off and put my dirty clothes back on. I felt like a new person.

I headed back to Anu's house, where we all had planned to gather for a farewell to Ang Lamu and their children. We stood in the main room as Ang Lamu presented us with bright white gauzy scarves called *katti*—gifts of friendship meant to bring good luck.

I looked at the faces around the room: the American faces of our climbing team, the faces of the Sherpas. We had been bound together for the past several weeks in a special friendship, through illness, hardship, and triumph. There had been very few disagreements and hardly a harsh word. We had been a real team. Perhaps the Sherpas had taught us something about graciousness, kindness, and compassion. They offered their friendship and opened their lives to us, just as they do for each other every day. The Sherpas get along with people so well because they respect themselves, each other, and even the foreigners who come to visit. Among the

Sherpas, it is a terrible disgrace for an adult to strike a child; and there are no police in the Sherpa villages because there is no violent crime.

Ang Lamu stepped forward, and I bent my head. Gently, she placed the veil-like *katta* around my neck. "You are very strong and very happy," she said to me. I raised my head.

"Thank you, Ang Lamu," I replied. "And I will find your American friends for you. *Namaste.*"

MOUNTAIN METHODS

Getting Along with Others— and Yourself

Mountain climbing is more than a physical challenge; it is a mental and emotional challenge as well. You have to keep a good attitude toward yourself and others on your trip as you make decisions and cope with the hardships of mountain climbing.

Choosing a Leader

If you are climbing with several friends and one is more experienced than the others, you might want to establish that person as leader. That way, when it comes time to make a decision or if there is an emergency, one person can organize the effort quickly. However, the leader should not be a dictator.

Disagreements

Chances are, you won't always agree with your climbing partners, especially on a long trip. Stress, physical discomfort, and fatigue can all contribute to flare-ups. When this happens, try to talk things out. If members of the party disagree over a decision, remember the bottom line: safety first.

Peak-Bagging

Some people like to reach the tops of as many mountains as possible, as fast as possible; these people are called peak-baggers. Peak-bagging doesn't really accomplish anything. You don't have to be first or fastest. The mountain will still be there, whether you are first in line or last. In addition, don't try to accomplish more than is reasonable in the time you have allowed for your trip. You could find yourself spending a night out when you didn't plan to, or you could run out of food and water, putting yourself in an emergency situation.

Fear

Climbing carries with it some fears: of storms, of falling, of getting lost, of wild animals, even of the dark. Don't be embarrassed about these; they are part of the challenge. When you feel these fears coming on, stop and think. Review your knowledge. Just thinking about all you know—about climbing safely, protecting yourself from the weather, and so forth—should boost your confidence and help you calm down. If you can, talk your fears over with one of your climbing partners. He or she may be feeling exactly the same way.

22

Namaste

WE SAILED DOWN the trail from Namche, *katti* flying, until the air became so gritty with dust that we stopped to unwind the gauze scarves from our necks, fold them, and place them carefully in our packs. Jim stayed behind in Namche for a few hours, trying to obtain a birth certificate for Ngorup, who didn't have one and needed it for his school in Kathmandu.

We clomped along, up and down, until we came to the curve where we had first spotted Everest, several weeks ago. We stopped and looked back one last time at the Goddess Mother of the Snows. The long plume of cloud fluttered like a *katta* from the neck of the mountain. We turned and continued down the path.

As we descended, Boyd's strength and power returned. By now he flew along, his feet thumping the earth, his long legs pumping. We were now around ten thousand feet above sea level, and as the air grew richer in oxygen, he grew stronger and stronger, until he was his old self.

Near the bridge crossing the Dudh Kosi, a sinewy man in a bright Lycra running suit skidded by us, murmuring "excuse me" and fleeing down the hill. He was a mountain runner: he had left Kala Pattar at 6:00 that morning and planned to arrive in Kathmandu in about three days. Mountain running is a sport popular among only a few people.

Midafternoon we left Sagarmatha National Park, passing by the station that had checked our trekking passes on the way in. As the afternoon light waned, we skirted deep green barley fields and brown, bare potato patches. We came to a long, elaborate sign announcing our arrival at the Japanese tea house where we planned to spend the night. This tea house has hosted many climbers and trekkers along the trail to Everest, and even boasts a modest library of mountaineering literature. We pushed open the gate and tromped up onto the wooden porch, where a table surrounded by benches and rickety chairs stood in full view of the trekkers moving by on the trail.

I shook my pack off my shoulders and sat down. Someone handed me a menu. I drew out my water bottle, gulping at it as I read the menu. One item caught my eye.

"Peach pie!" cried a high, wispy voice a few minutes later, and a boy with a birthmark the size and shape of a pointed beard on his chin brought me a fritter filled with peaches on a tin plate. I cut it open with my fork and the steamy, peachy odor was released. I was in heaven. Jimmy, Allen, and George arrived, all insisting on a taste of my peach pie. Convinced by a bite, they ordered their own.

At dusk, Jimmy organized a volleyball game with the Sherpas in the old potato patch next to the tea house, using a piece of twine for a net. They played with gusto, shouting and cheering, thwacking the ball back and forth, and diving for it as it fell toward the ground. We didn't know then that volleyball is a national pastime of the Nepalese. The yellow ball flew back and forth against the violet sky until it was too dark to play.

As we trooped inside for dinner, Jim arrived. We downed potatoes and vegetable curry by candlelight, crowded around a table gouged by camping knives. Later, we settled on hard bunks to sleep.

The next morning, Jettha, Dendi, and Kancha roped our gear to the yaks for the final time, as the animals milled around the patch where the volleyball game had been held. Then we clustered together for a group picture, including the yaks.

We set off down the trail in the dewy morning, headed toward Lukla. Up and down the familiar route we hiked, our feet moving as if they knew the way by themselves. As we neared Lukla in the afternoon, children ran up the trail from school, legs churning through the dust.

"Lukla?" I asked one girl.

She pointed over the hill. "Near," she replied.

As my legs worked up over the hill, a month's worth of fatigue swam through my limbs. In the distance, I heard the familiar howling of dogs. Soon we were there: among the open shops, trekkers bartering, chickens wandering through the streets, the whack of nails being driven into the boards of tea houses and lodges under construction. I stopped in a shop and bought a year-old chocolate bar. Then we made our way to the stone hotel next to the airstrip, where we had eaten our yak cheeseburgers on that first afternoon in the Khumbu, several weeks ago.

That night, our host, the owner of the hotel, served us dish after dish of rice, vegetables, different flavors of curry, and yak. We felt like royalty, seated at a smoothly veneered table on benches cushioned by embroidered pillows. He even had a tape recorder that played European rock music.

After dinner, we bundled up the clothing we planned to give to the Sherpas before leaving the next day. It's customary to give clothing such as pants, jackets, gloves, and hats to the Sherpas who have worked for an expedition. Warm clothing is very hard for them to get in their homeland. Later, we slept restlessly in sleeping bags on top of the beds in our hotel rooms. It seemed too foreign to try sheets and pillow cases.

The following morning dawned clear and crisp. We packed our gear for the last time, and Anu, Kancha, and Dendi dragged it off to the airstrip to be weighed for the flight to Kathmandu.

"They weigh our gear, but not us," explained Jim. "So wear all the hardware you can and string the rest around your neck and waist. That way, you'll have a better chance of getting on the plane."

Strewn about the hotel lawn, we yanked on our plastic mountaineering boots, flung harnesses loaded with carabiners and ascenders over our shoulders, and zipped on heavy parkas. Then we clomped up to the airstrip, where our Sherpas waited for us. We began our parting ceremony.

We presented our gifts of clothing to Dendi, Nima, Kancha, Pasang, Jettha, Kami, Dawa, Purba, and Zangbu. Each was so gracious it almost broke my heart. I wanted to be able to do more for them. I turned to Anu, my special friend. I handed him my snow gaiters. Then I said, "Here is a sweater for Ang Lamu. Thank her for having us in your home." He smiled his warm, toothy smile, and nodded. The Sherpas do not have a word for thank you, because it is not a special occasion when a person gives a gift or does a favor; it is simply part of normal life. To act kindly toward someone is the rule, not the exception.

"*Namaste*, Anu," I said, putting my hands together and bowing my head.

"*Namaste*, Linda," he replied.

Dawa disappeared and returned with long lengths of *katti*, which he slit with a knife and draped around each of our necks. I believed that these *katti,* and those that Ang Lamu had given us, would bring us the best of luck.

After gift-giving, we sat on the ground along the fence by the airstrip to wait for the two planes due from Kathmandu. We listened, tensed, for the siren that meant the planes had taken off from Kathmandu, flying toward Lukla. Time stretched. I read chapter after chapter of a book, not remembering anything I'd read. Two hours passed. Boyd grew restless and went off to the village to buy more chocolate bars. Time was running out; soon the clouds would shift from the Kathmandu Valley up to Lukla and we would not be able to get out.

Suddenly the short, sharp horn pierced the tension. Cattle were cleared and chickens were hustled away from the airstrip. Half an hour later, the tiny engine sputtered toward the dirt runway and the Twin Otter touched down, bouncing up the strip in a cloud of dust.

We grabbed our daypacks and Jim handed out pink boarding passes. We lined up for security check at a wooden booth with two stalls.

When my turn came, the security guard pointed to the empty stall. "Other room, please. For ladies," he directed. I stuck my head in the room.

"But there is no security person in there," I argued.

"Other room, other room, please." He waved me away. So I walked straight through to daylight on the other side. We huddled against the gate.

"Pink passes!" shouted the airline employee, and the gate opened. I glanced back at Anu, standing on the hill. Then we poured through the entrance, shoved our pink cards at the man with a clipboard, and jogged across the airstrip toward the plane. We ducked through the door and squeezed up the aisle and into seats. The pilot leapt into the cockpit and the hatch clicked shut. On the hill above the airstrip was a sea of Sherpa faces, a wave of Sherpa costumes.

The plane began to roll, bumping down the runway as it picked up speed. Jammed into the seats, we clutched our packs tightly to our laps. Later that day, we would send telegrams to our parents, rinse ourselves in hot showers, and gather at Jim's house in Kathmandu for a feast of roast chicken with stuffing and cranberry sauce, polished off with pecan pie. After returning to the United

States, I would learn that my real allergy was to anything with aspirin in it; those antacid tablets had been the culprits. Eventually, I would locate Anu's friends.

The Twin Otter soared off the cliff into the sky, and I gazed down from my window as we floated over Nepal, as serene as the jewel in the lotus. *Om mani padme hum,* the engine droned. It was Thanksgiving day, and we were headed home.

MOUNTAIN METHODS

When You Travel Far From Home

By now, you know that mountain climbing involves a lot more than just climbing the mountain. Sometimes it involves traveling, either to another state or to another country. Some tips may help you enjoy the traveling as much as the climbing.

1. *Learn about the place where you're going.* Try to read about the area surrounding the mountain: the people, their customs, local sights to see. If you're going to another state, write to the Chamber of Commerce of the town or towns near the mountain and ask for information. If you are traveling to another country, get a few books out of the library to read about the country. The more you know about where you're headed, the more you'll get out of the trip.

2. *Carry your passport.* If you are traveling to another country, you will need a passport and perhaps special visas, depending on the country. Apply for these a few months ahead, if possible. During your trip, carry your passport with you at all times, in a pouch attached to your belt or under your shirt. (That way, if you lose your backpack or duffel, you won't lose your passport.)

3. *Guard your money.* Don't carry a lot of cash. Instead, go to your bank and get travelers checks, which can be replaced if lost. Keep a record of the numbers of the checks in a different place from where you keep the checks themselves. Don't keep all your money and checks in one place; that way, if you lose some, you won't lose it all.

4. *Be a good guest.* Whether you are in another state or a foreign country, remember that you are a guest.

Respect the people who live there and their customs. By being nice, you may in turn make some new friends.

5. *See the sights.* If possible, take some time to see the sights of the region near the mountain. Try a local restaurant, visit a museum, ask about scenic views. People often like to talk about their town. When you've climbed your mountain, made new friends, and gotten to know the area, your climbing trip will be complete.

Glossary:
Tools, Techniques, Troubles, and Terrain

acclimatize   To let the body adjust to a higher altitude.

acute mountain sickness   A group of symptoms caused by exposure to high altitude.

altitude   The height of a place above sea level.

anorak   A parka or windbreaker.

ascender   A tool that attaches to the climbing rope and assists in the climb upward.

avalanche   A mass of snow, dirt, and ice that breaks loose and rushes down a mountain or slope.

backpack   A sack worn on the back to carry camping supplies; or to go on an overnight hike, carrying supplies in a backpack.

belay   To secure a climbing partner at the end of a climbing rope.

blaze   A mark cut or painted on a tree or rock to show the direction of a trail.

blister   A thin, round swelling of the skin, filled with water, caused by rubbing.

cairn   A pile of rocks used to mark a trail or route.

carabiner   An oblong metal clip with a spring gate used to attach ascenders and descenders to the climbing harness.

climbing harness   Straps made of nylon webbing that wrap around the waist and upper thighs, and attach to the climbing rope.

climbing rope   A special rope used by climbers to aid in climbing and help prevent a fall.

col   A pass between two mountain peaks; or a gap in a mountain ridge.

compass   A tool used to determine geographic location.

cornice   An outcrop of snow, like a hardened snow drift, created by high winds.

crampons   Metal spikes that attach to climbing boots to help grip snow and ice.

crevasse   A deep crack or gap in the ice of a glacier.

dehydration   Excessive loss of water from the body.

descender   A tool that attaches to the climbing rope and assists in the climb downward.

elevation   The height of a place above sea level.

false summit   A closer, lower summit blocking the true summit, or top, of a mountain.

fixed rope   A rope that is set in place by one climber for another to climb.

frostbite   The freezing of skin and the tissue beneath it.

gaiters   Cloth coverings that zip or snap around the ankles and lower legs to keep snow and dirt out of hiking or climbing boots.

glacier   A huge mass of slowly moving ice.

glacier glasses   Special sunglasses designed to protect the eyes from the strong rays of sun encountered on ice or snow.

glissade   A controlled slide, in either standing or sitting position, down a steep snowy slope.

heat exhaustion   The body's reaction to overheating, which includes salt-deficiency and dehydration.

heatstroke   A severe illness in which the body's temperature rises way above normal; also called sunstroke.

hypothermia   A serious condition in which the body's temperature drops way below normal; also called exposure.

ice ax A tool used by mountaineers for cutting steps, balancing, glissading, and breaking a fall on ice and snow.

icefall The face of a glacier, resembling a frozen waterfall; or an avalanche of ice.

ice screw A hollow metal screw used by climbers to anchor themselves or the climbing rope to a place on ice.

jumar An oblong clamp with a handle that attaches to a climbing rope and helps a climber ascend or descend the rope.

moleskin Padded tape used to prevent and treat blisters, especially on the feet.

moraine A ridge or pile of boulders, stones, and other debris carried along and deposited by a glacier.

mountaineering Mountain climbing.

nontechnical climbing Climbing in which a rope is not necessary.

pass A narrow gap between mountain peaks.

peak-bagging Reaching the tops of as many peaks as possible in the shortest amount of time.

pitch Distance equal to one length of climbing rope.

rappel A controlled slide down a mountain or cliff using a double rope.

ravine A deep, narrow gorge such as one through which a river flows.

scree Loose rock debris, especially on a steep slope or at the base of a cliff.

self-arrest The method by which a mountaineer breaks a fall using an ice ax.

snowfield An open slope of snow or glacier on the side of a mountain.

snowline The line between a snowfield and bare ground.

snowshoes Racket-shaped frames that strap to boots for use when walking in deep snow.

summit   The top of a mountain.

switchback   A trail that goes up a steep incline by zigzagging back and forth.

technical climbing   Climbing in which a rope is necessary.

traverse   To cross a slope or hillside.

tree line   The upper limit of tree growth on a mountain or at high altitude.

trek   To hike a long way. Trekkers are hikers.

Getting Started

Outdoor Organizations

There are many local outdoor organizations around the country that provide outings and/or instruction programs for young people. Check your school, YMCA or YWCA, Boy Scouts or Girl Scouts, or community center. In addition, the following organizations all have youth or student memberships.

Adirondack Mountain Club
174 Glen Street
Glens Falls, New York 12801
(518) 793-7737

Appalachian Mountain Club
5 Joy Street
Boston, Massachusetts 02108
(617) 523-0636

Colorado Mountain Club
2530 West Alameda Avenue
Denver, Colorado 80219
(303) 922-8315

Green Mountain Club
PO Box 889
43 State Street
Montpelier, Vermont 05602
(802) 223-3463

Sierra Club
730 Polk Street
San Francisco, California 94109
(415) 776-2211

The Mountaineers
300 Third Avenue, West
Seattle, Washington 98119
(206) 284-6310

Special Instruction Programs

National Outdoor Leadership
   School (NOLS)
Box AA
Lander, Wyoming 82520
(307) 332-6973

Outward Bound
National Office
384 Field Point Road
Greenwich, Connecticut 06830
(800) 243-8520

Equipment

In addition to your local outdoor-equipment store, the following firms have mail-order catalogs. Call or write to request a catalog.

Campmor
810 Route 17
PO Box 997-F
Paramus, New Jersey
  07653-0997
(800) 525-4784

Eastern Mountain Sports (EMS)
One Vose Farm Road
Peterborough, New Hampshire
  03458
(603) 924-9571

L.L. Bean, Inc.
Freeport, Maine 04033
(800) 221-4221

Recreational Equipment, Inc.
  (REI)
PO Box 88125
Seattle, Washington 98188-0125
(800) 426-4840

Maps

You can get many topographical ("topo") maps at your local out-door-equipment store. However, if the store doesn't have the maps you want, write to:

United States Geological Survey
  (USGS)
Map Distribution
Federal Center
Box 25286
Denver, Colorado 80225

Just in Case
(Your First-Aid Kit)

Your first-aid kit should contain the following things:

aspirin or Tylenol

medication for diarrhea

throat lozenges/cough drops

antiseptic cream

small bar of soap

Wash 'n Dry (or similar moistened towel)

sterile gauze pads (four inches square)

bandaids

adhesive tape

moleskin

elastic ("ace") bandage

small pair of scissors

tweezers (for splinters)

insect repellent

sunscreen

change for a phone call

Add additional items only if you know how to use them. Include medicines only if you are not allergic to them, and label all medicines clearly.

If possible, take a basic first-aid course at your local hospital, YMCA, YWCA, or school. Some of the organizations listed in "Getting Started" offer courses in first aid.

For Further Reading

Books

Look for these books in your library, local bookstore, or outdoor-gear shop.

Adventure

Arlene Blum, *Annapurna: A Woman's Place*

Chris Bonington, *The Everest Years: A Climber's Life*

Sir Edmund Hillary, *Ascent: The Autobiographies of Peter and Sir Edmund Hillary*

Sir Edmund Hillary, *High Adventure*

Sir Edmund Hillary, *Nothing Ventured, Nothing Win*

Louise Hillary, *A Yak for Christmas*

Louise Hillary, *High Time*

Showell Styles, *Mallory of Everest*

Joe Tasker, *Everest the Cruel Way*

Joe Tasker, *Savage Arena*

Julie Tullis, *Clouds from Both Sides*

Leonard Wibberly, *Epics of Everest*

Technique and Safety

Yvon Chouinard, *Climbing Ice*

Colin Fletcher, *The Complete Walker*

Peter Hacket, *Mountain Sickness*

Ed LaChapelle, *The ABC of Avalanche Safety*

Harvey Manning, *Backpacking One Step at a Time*

Ed Peters (editor), *Mountaineering: The Freedom of the Hills*

Royal Robbins, *Basic Rockcraft*

Magazines

Some of the organizations listed in "Getting Started" publish their own magazines. In addition, the following magazines have articles on camping, backpacking, and mountain climbing.

Backpacker

Climbing

Outside Magazine

Summit

About the Author

Linda Buchanan Allen has climbed mountains in the United States, the Swiss Alps, and the Himalaya. She is a trip leader and instructor for the Appalachian Mountain Club, teaching backpacking and back-country ski workshops. She has been writing material for young people for almost as long as she has been hiking. Her articles on travel and the outdoors have appeared in publications such as the *New York Times,* the *Boston Globe,* and *Appalachia.*

About the AMC

The Appalachian Mountain Club is a nonprofit, volunteer organization committed to conserving natural lands and promoting responsible public use of them. Founded in 1876, it is the oldest conservation and outdoor recreation organization in the country. AMC members were the first to explore and map many areas of the Northeast, and the Club played a vital role in the passage of the Weeks Act, which established the eastern National Forest System.

Activities.   Today the AMC conducts an increasingly varied program of outdoor public service. The Club's 35,000 members belong to twelve regional chapters stretching from Maine to Washington, D.C. Each month, chapter volunteers organize and lead hundreds of outdoor trips, workshops, and educational seminars. Club activities include hiking, skiing, climbing, snowshoeing, canoeing, trail building, cycling, and photography. Since 1968, the AMC has offered thousands of inner-city youths the chance to test themselves in the mountains and develop leadership skills through the Youth Opportunities Program. The AMC is also active in environmental research and land-management issues.

Facilities: The Club has built and now maintains many trails, shelters, and camps, a unique system of eight alpine huts in the White Mountains, and the base camp and information center at Pinkham Notch in New Hampshire. Club headquarters in Boston house the nation's largest mountaineering library.

Publications.   Beginning in 1907 with the *White Mountain Guide,* the AMC has published authoritative guidebooks and maps to the trails and waterways of the eastern United States. The Club also publishes in the areas of history, ecology, sociology, biography, backcountry management, search-and-rescue, and winter sports, as well as field guides and books for children. *Appalachia,* the nation's oldest mountaineering journal, is published twice a year.

Membership. We invite you to join the AMC. The monthly member's publication, *Appalachia Bulletin,* will keep you informed of Club news, activities, and conservation issues. All members receive discounts on publications and food and lodging in AMC facilities. Membership allows you access to AMC workshops, trips, and other activities, and gives you the satisfaction of supporting the preservation and responsible use of the Northeast's priceless open spaces.

For membership information, call us at (617) 523-0636, or write to:

Appalachian Mountain Club
5 Joy St.
Boston, MA 02108

NOTES

NOTES

NOTES

NOTES

NOTES

NOTES